I0812648

SECRET NEW YORK

HIDDEN BARS AND RESTAURANTS

Michelle Young, Laura Itzkowitz
and Hannah Frishberg
Photography: Alix Piorun and Augustin Paquet

JONGLEZ PUBLISHING
Travel guides

New York City has a wealth of hidden bars and restaurants, in part due to the city's Prohibition heritage and in part because New Yorkers need, and revel in, the urban escape. Beyond the craft cocktail movement that has taken New York by storm, we have attempted to encompass here the range of hidden locations in the city. The locations are as diverse as the city itself. From upscale Prohibition-inspired bars to dive bars, freight entrance food stands to gourmet supper clubs in hidden locations, from subterranean sake spots to a rooftop winter cabin, there is something for everyone in the hidden genre.

As a city built and rebuilt atop previous layers of history, New York City naturally lends itself to secret locations. At the peak of Prohibition, the city had 23,000 speakeasies – places where you could drink and had to "speak easy" to avoid detection. A few locations on this list are speakeasies from this time period, while many others ascribe to this contradictory era of both excess and regulation.

The definition of hidden requires some clarification, particularly for a city as dense as New York. Some places are literally hidden from view, down dark alleys or up seemingly private doorways. Other locations are hidden because they are difficult to find or easy to miss, but not deliberately. Still other locations have hidden activities – a Chinatown dim sum restaurant that becomes a nightclub, a bodega where you can pop a can of beer and eat tacos in the back, or a boutique donut shop inside a carwash. A small set of locations are pointedly exclusive, either by referral only or through the well-guarded sharing of a private phone number.

As is the nature of any guide, the process of publication ensures that new locations will be opened, and beloved locations may close. Places that were once hidden will suddenly add a large, obvious sign. But such is the nature of New York City, a city that is ever changing and always on the search for the new and the surprising.

Comments on this guide and its contents, as well as information on places not mentioned, are welcome and will help us to enrich future editions.

Don't hesitate to contact us: info@jonglezpublishing.com

CONTENTS

CONTENTS

GOVINDA'S VEGETARIAN LUNCH

Hare Krishna's vegetarian delight

305 Schermerhorn Street, Brooklyn, NY 11217
(718) 875-6217
facebook.com/govindaslunch
Monday to Friday 12pm–3:30pm
A, C and G trains/Hoyt-Schermerhorn St
Inexpensive

On the northern edge of Boerum Hill, Brooklyn, a large Hare Krishna temple stands as an anomaly, surrounded by dollar pizza joints and public welfare offices. Judging by the outside, you might never know that there's a vegetarian lunch canteen inside – a neighborhood spot unspoiled by guidebooks, most of which wouldn't be interested in such a modest, unglamorous place anyway.

But for Hindu devotees, neighborhood residents, and office workers, Govinda's is a convenient spot to get a cheap, healthy, and delicious vegetarian lunch in keeping with the Hare Krishna principles of nonviolence and service to god (Krishna) through vegetarianism. For the casual visitor, it's a window onto a small religious minority with a fascinating story.

Step inside and head down the stairs to the basement, where large round tables and metal chairs sit atop a clashing red and green linoleum floor. A small buffet station is set up at one end of the room, opposite a painting depicting the Hindu gods. The place looks like it has not been updated since its founding in 1982.

The decor is clearly not a priority, but that's not why you're here. You're here for the homemade samosas, roasted zucchini, tofu, and quinoa salad. The menu changes daily, and the cooks only serve fresh vegetarian food, both Indian and continental. A plate with your choice of three buffet items will leave you full for $6, and the proceeds support the temple.

The movement came to the United States in 1965, when 69-year-old A.C. Bhaktivedanta Swami Prabhupada arrived in Boston via freight ship to spread Lord Krishna's message in the West. Sent by his spiritual master in the holy land of Vrindavan, India, he had only $7 in change and a trunk of books on Krishna. He spoke at yoga studios, YMCAs, and bohemian artists' lofts, and often sat in parks playing a bongo drum and chanting the holy name of Krishna, gathering converts who believed in his teachings.

Govinda's canteen has been serving the community for the past six years. Before that, the staff only served meals after services, where devotees gather to chant the Hare Krishna Maha Mantra. Now, anyone is welcome.

GLASSERIE

Farm-to-table fare in a former glass factory

95 Commercial Street, Brooklyn 11222
(718) 389-0640
glasserienyc.com
Monday to Friday 5:30pm–11:30 pm; Saturday and Sunday 10am–11pm
G train/Greenpoint Av
Moderate

On the northernmost tip of Brooklyn, the cavernous building that once housed the Gleason-Tiebout glass factory remained empty for years because the landlord refused to sacrifice the building's integrity for another deli. When Brooklyn resident Sarah Conklin explained that she wanted to restore the building to a version of what it once was, he was excited about the project. "As soon as I saw the courtyard, I was done," she says. However, this place is not exactly easy to find – the majority of the clientele have sought it out. Outside, only a neon green G marks the entrance.

The courtyard hidden in the back is paved with cobblestones and partly open to the sky. The building goes back much further than the entrance would have you believe. When it was a glass factory, from the 1870s to the 1930s, the workers would cart their wares through the courtyard to the back exit, which opens directly onto Newtown Creek. They then loaded the glass onto boats to be shipped. Now, the factory's enormous kiln door hangs in the courtyard and an original ceramic basin holds plants. "I"m genuinely charmed by this place," Conklin says. "There's an architectural value that's really untouched."

As she prepared to open Glasserie, Conklin spent months researching. She found antique etchings of the factory's fixtures – now hanging by the entrance – through the Corning Museum upstate. Vintage pendants, bare bulbs, and cut glass fixtures each emanate their own special glow. Above the bar hang two lights from Paris subway stations circa 1890, with Art Deco details on the sides. Poised around the room are copper pots from Lebanon and Saudi Arabia, handed down by Conklin's mother.

Conklin is half Lebanese, and felt that those flavors were underrepresented in New York City. To say, however, that Glasserie serves purely Lebanese or Middle Eastern food would be to simplify it. The menu changes daily, as per the fresh produce and meats available from farms in the New York area, including Brooklyn Grange's rooftop. The real emphasis is on seasonal ingredients and honoring the integrity of the flavors. Syrian cheese brushed with Za'atar might be served with heirloom tomatoes in the summer and pickled beets in the winter. The eclectic wine list emphasizes obscure wines from the Mediterranean, Slovenia, and Croatia. A simple gin & tonic takes on a new character with saffron simple syrup, which brightens the palate.

SUNSHINE LAUNDROMAT

Not your average wash and dry ...

860 Manhattan Avenue, Brooklyn, 11222
(718) 475-2055
sunshinelaundromat.com
Monday to Friday 5pm–2am, Saturday & Sunday 12pm–2am

This is not your average wash and dry. The signs are clear from the front window, for those paying attention: Single sheets spell out the word "pinball," the letter "A" a sanitary inspection grade rating.

Inside, though, the non-attentive might still think all is suds as usual. Although there are a few pinball machines, the main room is mostly washers and dryers. But wait, what's in the vending machine by the front door? M&Ms and potato chips, sure, but also Plan B and a bottle of shampoo labeled "bacon." In fact, a few things are randomly labeled "bacon." And what's that hanging next to the perfunctory laundromat television? An odd and oddly varied amount of dog art. Strange!

And ho, what is through the windows of the two dryers at the end of the room? A whole second room, this one lacking in any laundromat fixtures beyond a change machine but equipped with a bar and completely lined in pinball machines.

In addition to the pinball, there's a coin-operated, fortune-telling, beer-toting chimp, a whole rack of board games, skee ball, a backyard and more.

The space became what it is thanks to two coin-operated fan boys' dreams: Peter Rose and Michael Medovy, whose father, Naum Medovy, bought Sunshine's building in the 1980s. The pair met when Rose came to sell and service equipment there in the early 2010s and became fond of the wash-and-dry. Eventually, Rose took over the lease, The New York Times reported in 2016, soon after the back pinball speakeasy room was completed.

Sunshine Laundromat's transformation into a hybrid laundromat-and-pinball parlor happened progressively. First, "I set up one pinball machine," Rose recalled to the Wall Street Journal in 2024, shortly after the bar reopened following a pandemic closure. Then, "Every few weeks, I would just rearrange furniture…remove a folding table, replace it with a pinball machine. A washing machine would become a pinball machine."

The shtick was a hit, but insufficient to contain Rose's entire pinball collection: In early 2025, Rose opened the nearby Scrappleland, at 1150 Manhattan Avenue, in the former space of Greenpoint Beer and Ale. Unlike Sunshine, Scrappleland has no secondary motive; it is purely a space for drinking and playing pinball.

For those who prefer to have a pinball and a beer with a side of detergent, though, Sunshine remains the end all and be all.

WEATHER UP

Classic cocktails and subway tiles

589 Vanderbilt Avenue, Brooklyn, NY 11238
(212) 766-3202
weatherupnyc.com
Daily 5:30pm–4am
2, 3 and 4 trains/Bergen St
Moderate

If not for the gleaming white subway tiles covering the façade, you might never even wonder what's behind the door of this little place on busy Vanderbilt Avenue. Venture inside, past the velvet curtain, and you'll find yourself in a glowing little jewel box of a bar. Amazingly, the white subway tiles continue on the inside, completely covering the ceiling, just like in the Paris métro. Yet unlike a grimy subway station, the place is outfitted in dark wood, brown leather, a copper bar, and marble tables. A wall-hanging made from an old piano adorns the front corner. Custom light fixtures made from thin slabs of stone hang above the bar, and little votive candles give the room a warm glow.

A Brit by birth, Kathryn Weatherup has worked in the service industry since she was 14 years old. After studying architecture, she ended up a bartender in Paris before coming to New York, so the echoes of Parisian design may not be a coincidence. It was there that she met designer Matthew Maddy, who's responsible for the look of the bar, which he transformed from a rundown gospel church into another kind of house of worship. Though Weatherup had been working in bars and restaurants for years, it wasn't until she tasted a true martini at Milk & Honey that she was finally bitten by the cocktail bug. Inspired by Sasha Petraske's return to the old-school way of making classic cocktails, she opened this little place near Prospect Park.

Petraske trained the staff, and it shows. Behind the bar, oranges, lemons, and limes sit in wire baskets, waiting to be pressed and blended with spirits and amaros. The short but sweet cocktail menu contains ten drinks – takes on the classics – but Weather Up's bartenders have the full repertoire of classic cocktails in their heads. Order a Vieux Carré (rye, cognac, vermouth, Bénédictine, bitters, and lemon) and you won't be disappointed. Try the Sir & Madam (gin, grapefruit juice, lemon juice, simple syrup, Peychaud's bitters, and sea salt) and you might just discover your new favorite drink. Should you be in the mood for something stronger, there's an absinthe fountain on the bar. You wouldn't be the first in this place to order yours on a drip. The bartenders, like Ben Curtis, are incredibly knowledgeable and friendly.

When the place opened in 2008, there were only a couple of other bars between here and Prospect Park. The formerly rough neighborhood has been changing steadily, and with the influx of more young professionals, Weather Up has gained a devoted group of regulars.

CELLAR AT ST. MAZIE BAR & SUPPER CLUB

Dine in a haunted cellar

345 Grand Street, Brooklyn, NY 11211
(718) 384-4807
stmazie.com
Daily 6pm–1am
L and G trains/Lorimer – Metropolitan
Moderate

Poised on the edge of Grand Street in Williamsburg, just before it drops off onto the Brooklyn-Queens Expressway, St. Mazie Bar & Supper Club is in a rather obscure location, but it's well worth the walk. Cross the threshold and marble café tables flanked by potted palms welcome you in. The wooden ceiling is curved, like the side of a ship, with rotating ceiling fans. Behind the bar stands a genuine 1920s refrigerator salvaged from a Buddhist monastery upstate. Toward the back, which resembles an old train car, wooden panels from a courthouse hem in the long, curved, leather banquette with tables and cane chairs. An antique sign for "Uptown Local Trains" hangs above. On a small stage in the corner with an upright piano beside it, musicians play gypsy jazz, swing, and flamenco on alternating nights of the week.

Every detail was meticulously chosen by John McCormick, who has had a hand in the design of several vintage-inspired neighborhood staples, including Maison Premiere, Five Leaves, the No Name Bar, and his own Café Moto (co-owned by Bill Phelps). He christened this place St. Mazie in honor of Mazie – just an old lady who watched after the Bowery's drunkards, really – profiled by Joseph Mitchell in the *New Yorker* in 1940. Here, she's been elevated to sainthood.

You could easily settle into the corner booth with a cocktail like the Gypsy (gin, Dolin blanc, and maraschino liqueur) and a platter of oysters, but then you'd be missing the real fun downstairs. An easy-to-miss door across from the bar opens onto a staircase that descends to the cellar – and that's where you'll really feel transported.

The dimly lit, low-ceilinged room was carved out by Italian stonemasons in the 1880s and served as a speakeasy and gambling den during Prohibition. With antique portraits hanging on the stone walls, rough-hewn wooden tables, and a small bar in the corner, it has the feel of an Old World wine cellar, like the ancient dank bars in the Parisian Latin Quarter. When you stand there, with the Django Reinhardt guitar strands reverberating through the wooden beams up above, you feel the forbidden excitement the people who came here to drink illicitly must have felt. Back then, this was a working-class neighborhood full of Italians and Eastern European Jews. Today, the owners insist there are ghosts haunting the cellar.

When John and his wife Vannesa opened St. Mazie, they intended the cellar to be its own thing: a supper club operating under the name St. Charles Cellar. They began serving a full menu focused on European comfort food, with favorites like roast chicken and slow-roasted porchetta with fresh herbs and spices. Though you can now get anything off the dinner menu upstairs in the bar, a meal in the cellar is a real treat.

HOTEL DELMANO

Old World sophistication in Williamsburg

82 Berry Street, Brooklyn, NY 11211
(718) 387-1945
hoteldelmano.com
Monday to Thursday 5pm–2am; Friday 5pm–3am; Saturday 2pm–3am; Sunday 2pm–2am
L train/Bedford Av
Moderate

Don't be misled by the name. Hotel Delmano isn't a hotel at all, though owners Michael Smart, Alyssa Abeyta, and Zeb Stuart were inspired by weathered hotel lobby bars. When they got their hands on this prime space on the corner of North 9th and Berry, they leapt at the chance to create a bar that they would want to hang out in. Their retro bar/music venue, Union Pool, opened in 2001 and at the time, Williamsburg's bars catered to a young, rowdy crowd. "I used to joke that people who graduate from Union Pool come to Hotel Delmano," Abeyta says. It takes a bit of effort to find though. The Berry Street entrance is gated off, so it looks like there's nothing there. The real entrance is around the corner on North 9th Street.

"We wanted a place where people could hang out and talk about poetry, music, or love, and not scream over the music," Smart explains. And so they built it. The name Delmano is a bastardization of *della mano*, Italian for "by hand." Over the course of a year, they renovated the space. They stripped the wallpaper, uncovering the original plaster and sealing it. Smart built the bar, the marble bistro tables, and some of the cabinetry. They sourced antique chandeliers, black and white photos, and an original 19th-century oil painting. A couple of rooms in back provide more intimate banquette seating under antique portraits.

"We built a place to escape reality and whisk yourself away," Smart says. Indeed, it's easy for locals and foreigners alike to feel swept away and yet familiar and comfortable. You'll find many goods by local purveyors: gin from Greenhook Ginsmiths, cheese from Murray's, and smoked fish from Acme. The wine list aims to surprise, straying away from conventional choices and showcasing small vineyards instead. Sherry is a personal passion of wine director Alex Alan, who lived in Spain. He has nothing but recommendations, and will be happy to help you choose from the twelve sherries served by the glass.

The cocktails – both house standards and seasonal drinks – are excellent. On the bar, you'll notice the glass bottles containing infusions prepared in-house. The head bartender works with the bar staff on new cocktail recipes. They collaborate, perfect their recipes, and present them to the owners. Sometimes people come in hoping to get a cocktail they had in the past, an amazing concoction with vanilla, apple, and cinnamon, let's say. The bartender can usually remember and recreate it, even if it's no longer on the menu.

MEXICO 2000 BODEGA

Taco stand inside a bodega

367 Broadway, Brooklyn, NY 11211
(718) 782-3797
Seven days a week 8:30am–10:30pm
J and M trains/Hewes St
Inexpensive

Mexico 2000 is a hole-in-the-wall bodega in South Williamsburg under the elevated J-M-Z train tracks that gave Jay-Z his name. It's called Mexico 2000 simply because it was opened in the year 2000. But more than your typical neighborhood bodega, Mexico 2000 serves up tacos and other Mexican fare in the back of the shop and is a rare one where you can drink as well. Simply grab a can or bottle of beer from the sliding fridge doors, which are within arms length of the handful of tables. Many Mexican imports are available like Tecate, Modelo, Presidente, and Pacifico, along with tall boys of Pabst Blue Ribbon and cans of Four Loko. Go with a small group or sit with the regulars at the tables, watching telenovelas on the small TV.

Mexico 2000 made its mark on the New York City culinary map in 2012 when Alex Stupak of Empellón made a dish inspired by the *chilaquiles* from the bodega. But fans of Mexico 2000 had been going there for years, picking up American and Mexican basics like plantain chips, sweet breads, lotto tickets, toilet paper, and canned foods from rickety shelves, while grabbing cheap, authentic Mexican food from the back.

Besides the famous chilaquiles, there are tacos, burritos, chimichangas, tortas, huaraches, sopes, enchiladas, tostadas, and more, along with soups and stews favored by the staff that are off the menu.

The location of Mexico 2000 is one of its most interesting traits, right along the border of three distinct communities: the Hasidic Jewish neighborhood south of Broadway, encroaching gentrifiers from the north, and the existing Hispanic community. This means that the clientele at Mexico 2000 is a little slice of New York City's diversity. You might also see musicians emerge from a basement studio beneath a graffitied building right across the street.

There are actually two locations of Mexico 2000 on the same block in South Williamsburg now. The success of the tiny bodega led to an expansion two doors down into a formal restaurant, taking over a long shuttered space that was once a bizarre nail salon. Still, the taqueria in the tiny bodega remains active despite the expansion, and Brooklynites should be grateful. Anything in New York City that still feels homegrown and local, hole in the wall or not, should be held on to.

LA MILAGROSA

An agave bar hidden behind a Mexican bodega

149 Havemeyer St., Brooklyn NY 11216
cerveceriahavemeyer.com
Wednesday to Friday 8pm–12am, Saturday 8pm–2am

Mezcaleria La Milagrosa in Williamsburg is hidden behind a freezer door inside a Mexican bodega – a front for the agave bar and listening room behind. The former space was once a laundromat, but it's impossible to tell in the intimate, hidden bar that feels like a mix between a forest cabin and a train car.

La Milagrosa is essentially an extension of Cerveceria Havemeyer next door, owned by chef and entrepreneur Felipe Mendez, though the two are not connected for the public. After hours, you'll find a hostess seated next to the freezer door, in front of an old-school red phone. It connects to another phone inside, where the bartenders pick up. The phone line is more than just for show, though: La Milagrosa is reservation only – no walk-ins.

Mendez is also a dedicated DJ who spins every Friday at Lot Radio (the station run out of a shipping container on an empty lot in Greenpoint) and the design of La Milagrosa reflects that. The top-of-the-line sound system, with McIntosh receiver and Klipsch speakers, is front and center at this bar, along with a DJ booth in the back that would have been a nook for guests in any other bar. Mexican tiles line the long bar and the curved ceiling enhances the acoustic sensibilities of the space. The freezer door is completely soundproof, truly concealing what's behind.

The friendly bartenders make a solid margarita, with a dash of Grand Marnier, as well as a "New Fashioned" with mezcal, orange bitters and cocktail sugar. You can order house made ceviches, supplied by the cerveceria next door, and the deli out front is fully operational, offering Mexican specialties, fresh-squeezed juice and coffee.

WYTHE HOTEL'S BASEMENT BAR

Bar hidden in Brooklyn's most famous hotel

80 Wythe Avenue, Brooklyn, NY 11249
(718) 460-8000
wythehotel.com
Open for special events
L train/Bedford Av
Moderate

When the Wythe Hotel opened in 2012, it was a major event for Williamsburg – some might even say a turning point. The formerly industrial neighborhood on Brooklyn's waterfront had been gaining a reputation as New York's next up-and-coming area for about a decade already, but the addition of a luxury hotel stamped its place as a destination equally as desirable as Manhattan. What's more, the former cooperage, built in 1901, was renovated with a distinct Brooklyn sensibility. The design preserved the building's shell and incorporated materials reclaimed during the construction process. Custom Brooklyn toile wallpaper – a cheeky take on traditional toile – was created for the guest rooms, and local artists like Steve ESPO Powers and Tom Fruin created murals and the iconic Hotel sign, respectively. The result is a thoroughly modern seventy-room hotel that honors its industrial heritage and the neighborhood's artsy character.

For locals as well as tourists, the Wythe Hotel quickly became a place to see and be seen. Its ground-floor restaurant Reynard (a project of renowned Brooklyn restaurateur Andrew Tarlow) is a local favorite for upscale farm-to-table fare. Ides, the rooftop bar, boasts stunning views of the Manhattan skyline and regularly has a line of people waiting to get in.

Yet few people who come to dine at Reynard or drink at Ides realize that there's a much more intimate bar hidden in the hotel's basement. This bar doesn't have a name and it's only open for special events. Down there, the hotel's historic character is even more evident. Exposed brick walls and vaulted ceilings make you feel like you might be standing in the cooperage's storage space for wooden barrels. Instead of casks, there are bottles behind the bar, black leather booths, and marble café-style tables.

The little basement bar is attached to the screening room, which hosts film festivals and other private parties. A small, windowless dining room in the basement with exposed brick walls, long wooden tables, and little chandeliers, becomes the backdrop for the Wythe Hotel's annual Halloween party. Revelers typically spill over into the adjacent bar. Though you can't wander in off the street hoping to get a drink there, anyone can rent the space for a private event.

BATHTUB GIN

Hidden behind a coffee shop but not secret anymore

132 9th Avenue, Chelsea, NY 10011
(646) 559-1671
bathtubginnyc.com
Seven days 6pm–2am; until 4am Thursday, Friday and Saturday
A, C and E trains/14th St
Moderate to expensive

Like Beauty & Essex in the Lower East Side, Bathtub Gin is a hidden bar in Chelsea that has capitalized on the speakeasy trend in New York City, run by a large restaurant group that knows how to hit all the right elements. You don't necessarily go to either of these places for the most authentic experience, but they are spots in the hidden bar vein that make things easy for larger groups. At Bathtub Gin, there's food, a big drink list, bottle service, live entertainment, and space. And it's well hidden.

Bathtub Gin is located behind a concealed door inside Stone Street Coffee Company, a roaster from Brooklyn with a tiny outpost on 9th Avenue. Come 6 pm, the coffee shop is filled mostly with people waiting to get into Bathtub Gin. Reservations can be made on OpenTable and the hostess is set up on the side of the coffee shop checking in guests and taking walk-ins, along with a bouncer who checks IDs.

The inside of Bathtub Gin is large with many different seating arrangements. There's a long bar lined with aperitivos and bitters and there's a row of high tables across from the bar. The main room has banquette seating on the sides with velvet damask couches. Chairs and settees form small groups in the center. The centerpiece of the bar is the copper bathtub with claw feet positioned perfectly for photographs and selfies.

The bathtub in general, a nod towards the days of Prohibition when booze was homemade in bathroom tubs, forms a central design element. You'll find smaller copper bathtubs as sinks in the restroom, another one on the bar functioning as an ice bucket and a tiny one as decoration close to the ceiling. The ceiling is tin, of course, and the floors are unvarnished wood. The damask pattern continues onto the wallpaper, which is adorned with a small collection of Prohibition-era photographs familiar to all, like the "We Want Beer" protesters.

Besides the cocktail list, which is arranged by liquor type, there are cocktails made from Bathtub Gin's proprietary small-batch rum developed in partnership with Mount Gay Rum in Barbados. It comes neat and on the rocks. The food menu ranges from small plates to larger dishes like duck confit or skirt steak. Cured meats and cheese plates round out the menu, plus desserts like chocolate truffles, crème brûlée, and toast your own s'mores. The most expensive item on the menu is the $1,075 bottle of Hennessy XO cognac.

RAINES LAW ROOM

Classic cocktails in a Victorian parlor

48 West 17th Street, Chelsea, NY 10011
raineslawroom.com
Monday to Wednesday 5pm–2am; Thursday to Saturday 5pm–3am, Sunday 8pm–1am
1, 2, 3, F and M trains/14th St
Moderate

You can't just open the door and walk into Raines Law Room. Like at the Prohibition-era speakeasies, you have to ring a doorbell and wait to be greeted. A man – looking suspiciously like a butler – will offer to take your coat and lead you through heavy velvet curtains into the parlor, for that's exactly what it appears to be. With sofas made of tufted velour, damask wallpaper, a fireplace, antique mirrors,

and vintage pictures framed in gold, the bar looks for all the world like a Victorian salon. The decor certainly facilitates conversations and romantic assignations. Four little nooks along both sides of the room were created by grouping two velour sofas to face each other, with translucent curtains separating them. Each nook can seat up to six guests, ensuring the group's intimacy, with a little service bell to ring when you'd like to order a drink.

Raines Law Room is a civilized place, but that doesn't mean you can't have any fun here. Open your leather-bound menu and you'll immediately see the story of Raines Law, which in 1896 prohibited the sale of alcohol on Sundays, except in hotels. All you needed for a hotel was a couple of shabby rooms to let above a saloon. Raines Law hotels started springing up like wildfire. Far from the intention, these little hotels were breeding grounds for prostitution and other societal ills. This cocktail bar's name is a cheeky nod to Raines Law.

The cocktails sprung out of the Milk & Honey school. Partner and head bartender Meaghan Dorman drank at Milk & Honey, Little Branch, and Death & Company when they first opened. At the time she worked at a restaurant in Harlem, but she was looking for somewhere that felt more like a home. She found Raines Law Room on Craigslist and was hired as one of the founding bartenders. "I think cocktails especially then were great for bringing out the geek in people," Dorman says. She used to pore over vintage cocktail books, reading them during her daily commute on the subway. She believes you've got to learn the rules before you can break them.

Michael McIlroy (formerly of Milk & Honey, now at Attaboy) trained the opening staff. All the hallmarks of a great cocktail bar are there: a wide variety of spirits, amaros, and syrups, fresh fruit and herbs and oversized ice cubes that won't dilute the drinks too much. The task of distinguishing Raines Law Room from its predecessors was left largely up to Dorman. She created a menu that grouped drinks together by their characteristics (shaken and refreshing, stirred and strong, a hint of spice, spritzes, and a page of staff picks). She hopes this will encourage people to try spirits they might not be as familiar and comfortable with, whether that means rye, cognac, or pisco. The bar, which you'll reach by walking through the parlor, resembles a kitchen, with a large sink, small refrigerator, and an island for prepping the drinks. Glass cabinets encase rare and expensive liquors as well as delicate antique glasses. Though there are no barstools, people often hang out back here when they want to chat with the bartenders, just as they would hang out with the host in the kitchen during a dinner party. Finally, don't miss the wallpaper design – it's not what it seems from afar.

THE TIPPLER

Follow a neon marquee announcing "Open"

425 W 15th Street, Chelsea, NY 10011
(917) 261-7949
thetippler.com
Tuesday to Thursday 5pm–midnight; Friday & Saturday 5pm–1am; Sunday closed

A favorite hangout among Google employees, The Tippler offers a den of college-bar energy with a masters-program tasteful decor.

Follow a neon marquee announcing "Open" to find this watering hole beneath the sprawling Chelsea Market complex. (For those who work for the tech giant, there's private access to the stairway which leads down to the bar.)

Like the market above it, The Tippler does a grand job of keeping it bright, cozy and inclusive in one of Manhattan's hottest real-estate markets: the focus here is not on self-serious, high-end decor and complex cocktails but tasty drinks and having a good time after work. Also, skiing …

"Both me and my wife skied in Aspen Colorado where after a day on the slopes everybody would meet at the local bar," says owner Michael Barrett. "We loved seeing people of all different walks of life come together and join in a night of fun. That was our inspiration for The Tippler."

Barrett designed the subterranean bunker of fun himself, doing his best to give it an "NYC feel." To achieve this, he decided to incorporate what, in his opinion, evokes New York more than anything else: a water tower.

"We found water-tower wood from a dismantled roof water tower in Brooklyn and built the bar top and surrounding shelves out of reclaimed water-tower wood," he says. Train rails from the High Line are also repurposed at The Tippler, which doesn't take reservations or have a dress code. It does, however, have a number of old newspaper boxes and a strange little shrine of sorts near the entrance as well as a photo booth in the back, by the bathrooms.

A backwards neon sign lamenting "wish you were here," an angelic ceiling mural, bar stools galore and rugs throughout complete the brick-heavy space's college-for-adults look. Columns wrapped in high-end fairy lights add to the aesthetic.

As for the menu, it's beer-heavy but also offers a number of booze-free drinks, a selection of house cocktails and just two food options: a salted soft pretzel and chips with salsa. Anyone hungrier is advised to "check out Chelsea Market" on the floor above.

Where the Oreo was invented

In another nod to NYC's industrial past – this one built-in – The Tippler's space happens to be part of the former National Biscuit Company (Nabisco) factory complex, which was built in the 1890s and redeveloped in the 1990s. It is here, in this self-same location where tech bros now join with tourists and other thirsty area denizens, that the Oreo was invented.

LOULOU

Ring the buzzer on the vintage Coca-Cola dispenser

176 8th Avenue, Chelsea, NY 10011
(212) 337-9577
loulounyc.com
Tuesday to Sunday 10:30pm–2am. Closed Monday

An aboveground French bistro serves as something of a red herring when it comes to locating this underground bar. The flower-festooned corner restaurant bears the same name as the speakeasy beneath it, but there's no way for customers to access the subterranean space by entering through the front door.

To get to Loulou's speakeasy space, walk around the side of the building to the red light and the alcove beneath it. Now ring the buzzer on the vintage Coca-Cola dispenser. If it's 10pm or later, you should be let in shortly.

The vending machine opens to a forested staircase leading down into a tricked-out former prep kitchen turned full-service bar full of jungle decor.

"The cheetahs were an accident," says Mathias Van Leyden, who co-owns both the above and below venues. While bedecking the intimate bar, the decorator – who did the job in exchange for credit and occasional use – happened to acquire a stuffed cheetah. That has since somehow become three stuffed cheetahs, two of which are now wearing hats gifted to them by customers, and all of which have acquired extensive imagined backstories. It's not the Chelsea cellar's wild cats who've become the two-story saloon's unofficial mascot, however, but a portrait of Leyden's rescue dog, Loulou, wearing a top hat.

Leyden was inspired to start the spaces – both named for his pooch – after two decades in NYC nightlife made him somewhat weary of maintaining larger venues. "I wanted to do a smaller version of what I've been doing for 20 years," he says of the two-tier, exotic ecosystem he's built on 8th Avenue (three tiers if you count the sprawling, lavishly adorned sidewalk sheds and seating).

Upstairs food can be ordered from below (staff take a set of employees-only backstairs down from the kitchen). Nosh options include daily oysters, shrimp cocktail and charcuterie boards as well as full meals, from duck leg confit to a yellowfin tuna sandwich and chicken paillard. The speakeasy isn't open for brunch but eaters at the main space can choose from Eggs Benedict, smoked salmon and croissant French toast.

Those who discover the bar behind the secret soda machine can enjoy not just drinks but, periodically, cocktail classes and live music. Diners upstairs get to enjoy the shows too – Leyden has rigged the sound system to pipe the tunes upstairs. "It's special," he smiles.

LA NOXE

A chic saloon within the subway

315 7th Avenue, Chelsea, NY 10001
lanoxenyc.com
info@lanoxenyc.com
Monday to Wednesday 6pm–1am; Thursday to Saturday 5pm–2am

This blink-and-you-miss-it subway speakeasy at one point had a 1,500-person waitlist. "We are basically hosting a nightly house party in our 28th Street underground living room," founder Jey Perie says of the vibe in La Noxe, the "discreet, sophisticated, sexy" operation he runs out of a 1-train station in Chelsea.

The 600-square-foot venue has two entrances: an aboveground, street-level one on 7th Avenue and the one which deposits guests at the bottom of the stairs on the southeast corner under 28th Street, just ahead of the turnstiled train entrance. Friends initially discouraged Perie from taking the space, doubtful he could find success in such a small hollow carved into the NYC underground.

After getting its liquor license the same day in March 2020 that coronavirus-induced shelter-in-place orders were announced for NYC, La Noxe spent the following 12 months in limbo, intermittently open, partially open and closed. Then, in March 2021, a viral TikTok video of its unusual location brought a stampede of customers who inundated the 30-person bar's reservation system, booking it out through the following year.

Part of the reason for the eye-watering waitlist is Perie's decision to only fill the space to 80 percent capacity, an attempt to give those with reservations, as well as the occasional curious straphanger, a little more breathing room while they enjoy their cocktails and small bites. The exclusivity appears to have done nothing but add to the intrigue of the little saloon in the subway stairs, with many guests making multiple attempts at walk-in entry, trying their luck again and again until they succeed in getting a drink at the tiny venue.

Once inside, the menu and decor are both significantly inspired by Perie's French roots and his time living in Tokyo and Barcelona. The bar has been carefully retrofitted with heavy velvet furniture customized to fit into the pocket-sized pub. Ferns, books and a vinyl library fill the corner beneath the only window – a paned looking glass into the subway just beyond – and underlit wall tops cast a sultry red glow on the rugs, arched banquettes and individual round tables which fill the rest of the room.

A barber shop, luncheonette, music studio and massage parlor are among the most recent former incarnations of this underground address, but it's now so full of plush carpeting and sumptuous armchairs that the ghosts of past businesses – as well as the hustle and grime of the subway mere inches beyond the black door – feel out of sight and out of mind.

THE FRYING PAN

A nautical brunch vessel

Pier 66 off West 26th St., Chelsea, NY 10001
(212) 989-6363
fryingpan.com
Daily 11:30am-11pm from April 1 to October 31

Permanently docked off Pier 66, the Frying Pan ship lived many lives before it came to be a nautical brunch vessel.

The United States lightship Frying Pan was constructed in 1929 to assist a too-petite lighthouse in warning mariners of the Frying Pan Shoals, treacherously shallow waters off the coast of North Carolina's Cape Fear. It did this for 30 years, from 1930 to 1964, with a break during World War II.

In 1965, it was decommissioned. In 1986, it sank.

Eventually, one Captain John Krevey got involved. Motivated by a dream of keeping New York City's working maritime history alive, he bought the Frying Pan and saw to its restoration. He scraped off all the barnacles, installed a new Volkswagen engine and, in 1989, sailed her to the boroughs, where he went about transforming her into a restaurant on the Hudson.

"Through a lot of trial and error, he was able to get permits," said his widow, Angela Krevy, recalling how her late husband, a Seattle native, "couldn't understand at that time why nobody was interested in the water in New York."

NYC's waterfront has been significantly revitalized since the 1990s, but the Frying Pan remains notable in offering not just waterfront but waterborne dining.

Today, it is a popular bar and eatery, open seasonally and for private events. Its menu leans into the nautical, offering fried calamari, shrimp ceviche, lobster rolls, and other seafood classics.

It offers both covered and completely al fresco dining areas across two stories. The interior, which is accessible only to staff, remains more or less un-updated, barnacles and all.

Docked aboard the ship, and perhaps offering a sense of scale, is an entire Erie Railroad caboose known as the Lackawanna Railroad Barge, which was purchased to help dock the Frying Pan, and now lives atop it.

Adjacent to the Frying Pan is another ship, the retired FDNY Fireboat John J. Harvey, which periodically goes out on free public trips. Both vessels are historically designated.

In addition to her main and namesake location, the Frying Pan also has two landlubbing sister locations: Frying Pan Brooklyn and Pier i Cafe.

APOTHEKE

Apothecary-themed speakeasy

9 Doyers Street, Chinatown, NY 10013
(212) 406-0400
apothekenyc.com
Seven days a week 6:30pm–2am
J, M, Q and Z trains/Canal St
Moderate

Doyers Street in Chinatown was once called "The Bloody Angle" because the curvilinear road enabled gangs to creep up on one another unseen. Today, at that precise bend of the street is an apothecary-themed speakeasy, aptly named Apotheke. Located in a space formerly occupied by a karaoke and dumpling bar, the only sign that marks the location says "Chemist." The perpetually gated windows are filled with medicinal jars, while an imposing European oak door has a small eyehole. Inside, the bar opens up onto a spectacular old-world inspired space. Above a reclaimed wood floor intermixed with porcelain tiles, the original tin ceiling was discovered under two feet of soundproofing during renovation.

The bartenders wear lab coats (except on Prohibition Wednesdays), serving up a seasonally changing menu with a holistic, "farm to bar" approach above an illuminated bar made from Carrera marble. As such, the ingredients come from New York City greenmarkets, organic vendors, and their own rooftop garden, along with local Chinatown markets and shops. The cocktail menu is organized into sections referencing medicinal remedies like painkillers, stimulants, aphrodisiacs, stress relievers, and euphoric enhancers – liquid prescriptions, essentially. There is also absinthe, prepared the traditional way with sugar and ice-water drip, house-infused cocktail pitchers, and a selection of wines and champagne. Because of the constantly evolving menu, the bartenders get a chance to create new drinks that can be elected to the menu.

Pharmaceutical references are embedded throughout the decor. The chandelier and light fixtures are actually chemistry beakers filled with absinthe. Antique medicine bottles, collected from around the world, are filled with items like phosphoric acid and mustard seed. The wall pattern features a play on the Greek medicinal symbol as well as the organic chemistry of herbs and elixirs. Nods to the Prohibition era are also present throughout – a vintage alcohol still is transformed into the spout for the bathroom sink while an industrial sugarcane press sits in a corner.

Behind the banquette seats you may notice alcoves and archways in the exposed brick wall. These were the original windows of the building, with the bottom half of the openings now buried under landfill. It gives you a sense of how much of the land has been filled in Chinatown and why the rumors of hidden tunnels still persist. In fact, just next door is the entrance to one of those tunnels that enabled some gang escapes in the early 20th century. Enter the tunnel on Doyers Street and pop out in Chatham Square after walking through a fascinating little world of feng shui, reflexology shops, law firms, and travel agencies.

ATTABOY

New York's most legitimate speakeasy

134 Eldridge Street, Chinatown, NY 10002
Daily 6pm–4am
B and D trains/Grand St
Moderate

When Sasha Petraske moved Milk & Honey to its Flatiron location, two of his protégés, Michael McIlroy and Sam Ross, set up Attaboy in its place. It might be the most legitimate speakeasy in New York right now. There's no phone. There's no website. When you find the address, all you see on the door is "AB 134. Please Knock Gently." Next to the door, there's a small doorbell with the prompt "Ring Buzzer," as if it was an apartment. Look up and above the door you'll see a closed-circuit camera. Inside, the host and bartenders can see you on a small TV screen behind the bar without relying on the old Prohibition-era peephole. Here, the camera sees all. Don't bother trying to open the door because it's locked. You have to wait for the host to swing open the door, look you over, and decide if he has room for you or not. This may seem terribly pretentious, but with such a tiny space, they simply can't allow overcrowding.

Inside, the place looks much like it did when it was Milk & Honey. The interior is about the width of a train car, with a long narrow bar taking up the front, and a few booths in back, lit (though just barely) by spherical pendant lamps. The whole place can only fit about forty people, with a maximum of eighteen in the booths. The walls are exposed brick. The window facing the street is frosted over, so from the outside you can't see in, but from the inside you can see a faint light filtering in and old lettering.

The booths offer enough privacy that you can focus exclusively on the people you've come with. The best seat, however, is right at the bar, close to the bartenders. Only a couple of bartenders can squeeze back there at a time, but they manage to stir and shake enough cocktails to keep everybody happy. There's no menu, but the bartenders have a thorough enough repertoire of classic cocktails (and variations on the classics) to keep anybody guessing no matter how many drinks they've had and how many times they've been there. They don't stock vodka, but if you don't know that and you ask for it, they'll politely steer you toward gin, and that could go in any number of directions. The Diamond Fizz, a take on the classic Gin Fizz, is concocted from gin, lemon, egg whites whipped into a frothy foam, and champagne.

All the cocktails are prepared with as much thought and dedication as at any other bar in the Milk & Honey school. Yet at the end of the day, these guys are very down to earth. You get the feeling you could talk to them for hours – and maybe you do. The bar is open until 4 am every night, and late nights tend to become a who's who in New York City's cocktail bar scene. Many of the bartenders from the other venues included in this book list Attaboy as their favorite hidden bar.

SAINT TUESDAY

A jazz bar in a hotel's sub-basement

24 Cortlandt Alley, Chinatown, 10013
sainttuesdaynyc.com
sainttuesdaynyc@gmail.com
Daily 6pm–2am

Down and deep beneath one of NYC's only true alleys, Saint Tuesday requires quite a bit of climbing to access. Located below Tribeca's trendy Walker Hotel, the bar offers an industrial chic respite for those who descend a back stairwell into the catacomb-like depths.

The bar is open and features live music seven nights a week, the performances a cheery contrast to the exposed brick-and-beam surroundings. The tunes vary from gypsy jazz to Brazilian choro while the cocktail recipes have a pared-down, simple focus meant to emphasize fresh ingredients over wide variety. The proudly brief menu includes $20 classics (Manhattans, Old Fashioneds, Negronis), high-end alcohol takes on traditional mixes using vintage spirits, and a few more unusual options, including the Glass House (gin, aperol, fresh lemon, cucumber) and the Leo Season (tequila, fresh lime, orange, cayenne).

The intimate environment, general mixed-upedness of drinking, and coming upon a band in a Tribeca sub-basement prove a winning combo. The space is genuinely elevated and feels like much more than just another hotel bar.

A set of house rules, though not aggressively enforced, sets the mood as being more about good times than exclusivity. They renounce all "name dropping," "talking about fighting" or bringing down unfamiliars. Most importantly, they ask that patrons "exit the bar briskly and respectfully. Hotel guests are trying to sleep above." And while entrants are often led down into the bar's abyss, they are frequently left alone, finding their own winding way back up to the world above.

Saint Tuesday's ambience is intended to give "the feeling of a Parisian jazz cave" but one that is "quintessentially New York," says Christopher Covey – who headed up the bar's cocktail program. Although a jazz cave, it's not of the jazz age, he adds, explaining that he attempted to reconjure not that popular time period at Saint Tuesday's but instead the "Titanic era, a bit more working class and rustic, with an ice box behind the bar from the late 1800s and wood floors pulled from a barn upstate."

That atmosphere pairs well with the scenic alley above (a popular film location used in countless movies) and the long walk down into the lodge's belly. Perhaps most fitting with Covey's vision is the sheer depth of the location beneath the street – it's the flourescent-lit journey down the barely touched-up stairs that makes the experience feel so disorienting. And, overall, Covey says he has striven to achieve a place where guests can briefly "feel unstuck from time and space, where they can spend 20 minutes or three hours and still feel that with the setting and cocktails, they are able to be transported, even if only for a brief while."

TAAM TOV

Above the world's largest diamond district

Taam Tov: 41 West 47th Street, 3rd floor
Diamond District, NY 11036
Monday to Thursday 10am–9pm, Friday 10am to before Sabbath,
Sunday 11am–6pm
Transport B, D, F and M trains/Rockefeller Center
Moderate

It is estimated that over 90% of the diamonds that enter the United States come through New York City, the majority through one block on 47th Street. There are shops upon shops of diamond dealers, gold buyers, and jewelry polishers. Hawkers on the street aggressively seek buyers and sellers, and amidst these are men advertising a restaurant on the block : El Rincon del Sabor, an Ecuadorian restaurant hidden on an upper floor.

The cuisine choice makes sense for the main clientele, the 23,000 workers who make a living on the block. The Diamond District, formed in Midtown in the years before World War II, grew in importance during the war as Jewish diamond dealers fled to New York. Behind and above the façade of diamond stores on the ground floor are the Hispanic and Chinese laborers who set and polish the jewelry.

Taam Tov has been on 47th Street for over ten years, owned by a group of individuals from Israel and Uzbekistan. Enter through a narrow staircase, and pass the first and second floors. On the third floor, you'll first come across a takeout window, with delivery men on the stakeout for the next order. Just down the hall is the entrance to the restaurant. The glatt kosher food is Bukharian in origin, with specialties like Uzbek pilaf, beef stroganoff, and *bakhsh*. Also available are shish kebabs, steaks, lamb chops, traditional soups, and ten different types of salads. A must-have is the *lepeshka*, the Uzbek homemade bread paired with an order of *baba ganoush*. The food is delicious – a balance of simple ingredients packed with flavor.

Despite the spartan decor, El Rincon del Sabor is a place for leisurely lunches. The hidden nature of this spot ensure that the experience of eating in the Diamond District continues to reflect the unique ethnic breakdown that make up this dense business district.

SUNKEN HARBOR CLUB

Something entirely different

372 Fulton Street (2nd floor), Brooklyn, NY 11201
sunkenharbor.club
info@sunkenharbor.club
Daily 5pm "til late"

From 1879 to 2004, the eatery Gage & Tollner offered Brooklynites a white tablecloth experience and earned the unofficial honor of being the borough's arguably most famous restaurant. Then, one solemn Valentine's Day, after 125 years in business, the eatery served its last meal and descended into a 12-year period of assorted incarnations up to 2016: a fast-casual restaurant, bargain retailers, Arby's and TGI Fridays all varyingly called the Fulton Street address home.

Skip to 2021 and, after years of renovations and an additional pandemic delay, the fabled institution reopened under the former name, now an oyster and chop house with a separate bar above.

The downstairs revival successfully brought back the space's old 19th-century glamor with the restoration of its Gilded Age dining room – only the third NYC interior to achieve landmark protection after the New York Public Library and Grant's Tomb – and electrified gas-light-era chandeliers.

Meanwhile, upstairs, a tasteful but tiki-themed institution named Sunken Harbor Club has done something entirely different. Here, in place of arched mirrors and golden wallpaper, there are plush red booths, a backlit window of an underwater scene behind the bar, wave sounds gliding gently behind the music and seven dining tables hand-painted with different vignettes from an 18th-century Dutch work about rare sea creatures. Tropical fish from Louis Renard's 1754 *Histoire Naturelle des Plus Rares Curiosités de la Mer des Indes* are found on the bar's postcards, its coasters, its menu and in "every corner of the Club," according to a post by the pub.

The bar offers its own brief menu independent of Gage & Tollner. It runs the gamut from ramen and dumplings to ribs and salt-cod fritters. Also different from the downstairs eatery, which books out months in advance, Sunken Harbor does not accept reservations and both bar seats and tables are available on a first-come, first-served basis. (Gift certificates work at both venues.)

Although the cocktail menu is most easily labeled as tiki, it is also inspired by the travel writing of 20th-century culinary writer Charles H. Baker, Jr. and "cutting-edge mixological" techniques. These "molecular" methods include the high-pressure flash-infusion of spirits, acid adjustments and forced carbonation.

Before putting down anchor with Gage & Tollner upon the restaurant's reopening, Sunken Harbor Club spent eight years as a successful, nautical pop-up concept at the Red Hook bar, Fort Defiance. Both bars are owned by one St. John Frizell.

To reach the Harbor, guests must enter through the restaurant downstairs.

KARASU

"It was never meant to be hidden. It just so happens that the space dictated that."

166 Dekalb Avenue, Brooklyn NY 11217
(347) 542-8627
karasubk.com
Monday to Thursday 5pm–11pm, Friday and Saturday 5pm–12pm, Sunday 5pm–10pm

Fort Greene's moody izakaya Karasu wasn't initially planned as a speakeasy.

"It was never meant to be hidden. It just so happens that the space dictated that," explained restaurateur Danny Minch.

He and his fellow Karasu co-owner Dylan Dodd had opened the classic American eatery Walter's in a sunny corner space across from Fort Greene Park in 2011. A few years later, the landlords approached the pair about the fact that the chiropractor who'd been operating behind Walter's was leaving – did they want to take over the space?

"We just signed the lease and had no idea what we were gonna do in the space" except that it shouldn't compete with Walter's, said Minch.

Eventually they decided to turn it into a Japanese whisky bar, but as they were building out the watering hole, they came to feel that it also warranted a dining experience.

Karasu – "Little Crow" in Japanese – finally opened in 2016.

The menu invites customers to stay all night, or for just a round. There are Japanese-influenced artisan cocktails that are heavy on the yuzu and whisky, as well as a full sake menu. Food items are all intended for sharing, and include lighter bites – wagyu short rib, chilled soba, salmon croquettes – in addition to full meal fare: Ikura Don, a cauliflower steak and a 22 oz. prime ribeye, among other choices.

To access Karasu, diners must walk through Walter's to the very back, where a black door hardly beckons away from the lively bistro (indeed, it's barely visible). Behind it sits a dimly lit, alluring space with a black-paneled ceiling and only a skylight to remind patrons that the rest of the world exists beyond Karasu's walls.

"We really tried to build a space that allowed you to kind of forget about whatever's happening outside," said Minch, "a more intimate space where you don't know if it's day or night, the time of year, any of that stuff."

The bar is so successfully removed from reality, Minch added, "A lot of our regulars at Walter's that have been coming there for the last 14 years, some of them just pop back there and say, 'I never knew this existed.'"

DEATH & CO

Cutting-edge cocktails in a dimly lit den

433 East 6th Street, East Village, NY 10009
(212) 388-0882
deathandcompany.com
Sunday to Thursday 6pm–1am; Friday and Saturday 6pm–2am
F train/2nd Av
Moderate

There are few places in this city where booze is more loved (and consumed). At Death & Co, a small seating-room-only cocktail bar hidden in plain sight on a quiet street in the East Village, over 200 bottles line the back bar, lit from behind as if spotlighted on a stage. Besides the backlit bar and some candles on the tables, the place is almost pitch black. Sitting in one of the low booths, you feel completely enveloped by the darkness, as if the outside world is a distant memory. But before you can get inside, you have to give your name and party size to the bouncer at the door. If there's a wait for a table, he'll take your number. There's almost always a wait – sometimes an hour or more.

You might be wondering: Why on earth would anyone wait over an hour just for a drink? Because at Death & Co, it's not just a drink – it's an experience, and it starts the moment you approach the door. Once inside and seated at a table, a server will bring you a glass of water and the menu – more of a book, really, with a minimum of fifty cocktails listed at any given time. When you finally decide what to order, you can expect to wait longer than you normally would. Be patient. Death & Co's cocktails typically have four to five ingredients, including fresh-squeezed juices, rare amaros, spirits, cordials, and aperitifs. Each drink is prepared with a particular method (stirred with a long metal spoon, shaken in a Boston shaker, strained with a Hawthorne strainer), and served in a specific type of glass. All the recipes have been vetted by the owners and the bartenders, who are certifiable cocktail geeks, so you know they're going to be good.

The duo behind Death & Co, Dave Kaplan and Alex Day, quickly earned a reputation as among the best in the business – a fact they credit to their excellent team. Some of the best bartenders in New York have worked here, and several have gone on to manage other elite bars. "Our best bartenders have dizzyingly brilliant minds. They could be doing anything," Kaplan says. "They're here because they really want to be here." Whenever they get a new bottle, they research its history and origins, what it's typically combined with, and how it reacts to being manipulated.

The whole venture was a bit of an experiment. After working in the service industry for much of his life, and managing a bar in Las Vegas, Kaplan came to New York City knowing only what he *didn't* want to do. Death & Co was a reaction against the flashy, over-the-top bars of Vegas: it's intimate, dark, and earnest with an emphasis on fresh, handcrafted cocktails. Inside, there are no windows or clocks. "If we're doing our job right," Kaplan says, "you lose track of time."

DECIBEL

Grungy underground sake bar

240 East 9th Street, East Village, NY 10003
(212) 979-2733
sakebardecibel.com
Monday to Saturday 6pm–3am; Sunday 6pm–1am
6 train/Astor Pl
Inexpensive

This little sake bar is not the kind of place that people wander into during a night of barhopping, but it has a dedicated cult following. First you have to find the entrance, with a small sign and a little dormer roof poised above a dubious-looking staircase that leads down into the basement bar. Then you have to make it past the Japanese bouncer guarding an actual rope hung across the waiting room. "Are you meeting friends?" he'll ask, making you wonder if you were supposed to make a reservation. But no, they don't take reservations. They just need to know how many people you're with, so they can find a table for you. There's no standing room, so unless you arrive very early or late, you'll probably have to wait.

Once you get past the rope, you'll cross a short corridor and enter a dark room with a small bar, a couple of booths, a handful of tables, and decorations like a Maneki Neko (the ubiquitous lucky cat). A couple of large Japanese paper lanterns give off a warm glow, casting light on the walls, which are completely scrawled over with graffiti-style messages from past patrons. Though owned by Bon Yagi (the owner of Sakagura), this place feels completely different – like a debauched underground drinking den down a dark alleyway in Tokyo. It's a favorite among the owners of some fancy cocktail bars in the neighborhood.

The bar stocks almost a hundred kinds of sake, with a huge range in price and quality, some served warm, others chilled. There's Japanese beer (Sapporo, Asahi, etc.), plum wine, *shochu* (a distilled spirit with a slightly sweet, nutty flavor), and rare Japanese whiskeys like Yamazaki, which are becoming more popular with bartenders and whiskey aficionados. They serve traditional Japanese bar food too, like sashimi, shumai, okonomiyaki, udon, and soba, which pair nicely with the booze and will help you avoid getting sloppy. By the time you wander back onto the street, you might be surprised to find yourself in the East Village instead of Tokyo.

NUBLU

Nonconformist music haven and club that sometimes offers secret shows

62 Avenue C, East Village, NY 10009
(347) 529-5923
nublu.net
F train/2nd Av
Moderate

During the day, the outside of Nublu looks like a shuttered storefront, with metal grates perpetually down except for where the slats have broken off. Sometime between 2013 and 2014, street art appeared which added a splash of color to this otherwise discreet spot in Alphabet City. At night, the only sign of something happening is the little blue light marking the entrance. Inside however, activity is truly buzzing, as Nublu has become a stronghold for musical improvisation across genres. Colin Kasprowicz, a New York-based DJ and musician who regularly performs at Nublu, describes it as "Alphabet City's underground, nonconformist forward-thinking music Mecca."

Nublu had humble beginnings in 2002 as a simple clubhouse where friends of owner Ilhan Ersahin would come and play music. Ersahin, himself a musician on keyboard and the saxophone, describes its early days as more of a rehearsal space. He acquired the wine and beer license just so they could drink during and between jams, as the space was always open to the public. It's a haven for musicians getting their careers started, as well as for famous ones like Moby, Norah Jones and David Byrne, who come to perform secret shows or take in the latest sounds. Moby has said that he "had more fun DJ'ing records for seventy-five people at Nublu than going on tour and performing for 10,000 people a night." Celebrities like Kevin Spacey can sometimes be seen at the bar – it's one of those places you go to for music and inspiration, a place where everyone can do exactly what they feel like. Next to the casual drinkers at the bar may be someone solo dancing up a storm, but it all works.

More than just a club, Nublu is also a record label, which launched in 2005. It's hard to define the music exactly, as the Nublu label is more about curating taste with its roots in beatnik subculture. There's the rhythmic dance music of Brazilian group Forro in the Dark, the jazzy trip-hop of early group Wax Poetic (who had Norah Jones as a vocalist), the experimental Nublu Orchestra, along with electronica artists from the New York area and abroad. Most recently launched is the Nublu Jazz Festival in New York City, Rio de Janeiro and Istanbul.

At the bar, expect a wide range of sake, along with beers and wine. Nublu will eventually move down the street, below Studio 151, a fairly hidden recording studio and bar also run by Ersahin. The old space will stay in Ersahin's hands but might be something totally unexpected, as is to be expected from Ersahin, with a sushi place being considered.

PLEASE DON'T TELL

Through a vintage phone booth

113 St. Mark's Place, East Village, NY 10009
(212) 614-0386
pdtnyc.com
Daily
L train/1st Ave; F train/2nd Av
Moderate

Please Don't Tell (or PDT as insiders know it) is one of the more memorable speakeasy-style experiences, mainly because you enter

it through a vintage phone booth in a hot-dog shop. For first-time visitors, this is quite astonishing. Coming in off the street, you walk four steps down into Crif Dogs, a divey little hot-dog place with a fast-food style counter, a few tables, and arcade games. Just to the left is a vintage phone booth. Slide the door open, pick up the receiver of the red rotary phone, and dial 1. A hostess will answer and grant or deny you entry by opening a door on the other side. The process is certainly reminiscent of a speakeasy – if you have an "in" (a reservation will do) you'll be admitted, but if not, you might be told to wait.

Inside, the contrast between the shoebox-sized bar and Crif Dogs couldn't be greater – a fact the bar has capitalized on. PDT is dimly lit and done up in the style of a 19th-century tavern, with a low ceiling fashioned from diagonal wooden slats, a few black leather booths, a long copper bar, and taxidermy-adorned brick walls. If you sit at the bar, you'll be packed in tight, but you'll have the best vantage point to see what the bartenders are mixing up. Jim Meehan, the bar's co-founder and partner behind the cocktail program, is a self-declared cocktail geek. He wrote the "PDT Cocktail Book", edits Food & Wine magazine's annual cocktail book, and is the Drinks Editor of Tasting Table. Under his guidance, PDT won the James Beard Foundation's inaugural Outstanding Bar Program award in 2012. Though he no longer lives in New York City, his influence can still be felt.

At any given time, the menu features a list of 18 cocktails. Every few months, a couple are switched out and others are introduced, tied loosely to the seasonality of the ingredients. Bottles are lined up in front of the mirrored backbar, and glasses, tools, bitters, and garnishes are kept within easy reach, so bartenders won't be slowed down looking for things. There's a certain theatricality to the way they stir and shake drinks – sometimes several at a time – which can only come from mastering the techniques. Dressed up in suits and ties, they certainly look the part. The bar serves hot dogs from Crif Dogs, including some special recipes by high profile chefs David Chang, Wylie Dufresne, and Daniel Humm.

PDT has garnered a lot of press in New York City and around the world, so it caters to a large tourist population, especially on weekends. Weeknights are calmer and see more locals and industry people coming in to talk shop. What most people don't know is the bar's creation story. Co-owner Brian Shebairo opened Crif Dogs first and got a liquor license before the East Village's community board made them more and more difficult to get. When he and Jim Meehan opened PDT in 2007, they avoided applying for a new liquor license by putting the bar on the same property as Crif Dogs, without a separate street entrance. Thus this speakeasy was born.

THE RED ROOM

Jazz Age speakeasy above KGB

85 East 4th Street, East Village, NY 10003
(212) 787-0155
redroomnyc.com
Friday and Saturday 9:30pm–2:30am and for private events
F train/2nd Av
Moderate

There's nothing secret about KGB Bar, the Soviet-inspired literary outpost in the East Village. Writers – both esteemed and unknown – have been doing readings there for over 20 years. But The Red Room above KGB, which traces its roots back to Prohibition, is another story.

Outside on the street, a neon sign announces KGB, but there's no indication of the Red Room. The building on East 4th Street that houses both bars, as well as the Kraine Theater, was built in 1858 and briefly housed the Women's Aid Society. In the '50s and '60s, the Ukrainian Labor Home, a social club for Ukrainian socialists, occupied the building. They hosted banquets on the first floor and operated their own private speakeasy on the second floor. But before the Ukrainian Labor Home bought the building in 1948, notorious gangster Lucky Luciano ran a speakeasy called the Palm Court there.

Today, The Red Room on the third floor operates as an event space and speakeasy of sorts. Though most people climb the narrow marble stairs only up to the second floor, if you keep going up, you'll find an unmarked red door with a gold Art Deco peephole. Cross the threshold and you'll find yourself in an intimate bar where the decor and cocktails are throwbacks to the 1920s. Owner Dennis Woychuk, a native New Yorker, restored the tin ceiling and brought in period decor, like the Art Deco wall sconces from a Detroit movie theater. He has been involved with the building since 1983, when he operated an art gallery in what is now the Kraine Theater. As a kid, he used to come to the Ukrainian Labor Hall with his father. He had his first taste of whiskey there at the tender age of five.

While KGB hosts literary readings, The Red Room hosts 1920s bellydancing shows, live jazz, and private events. At the front of the room, a small red-curtained stage is set up for intimate performances. The music is enough to transport you to a timeless New York, where strangers become friends over a round of drinks and time inches on toward the wee hours of the morning. Settle in with a Gin Rickey – F. Scott Fitzgerald's favorite – a French 75, or a champagne cocktail with Angostura bitters. One too many and you might end up in the big copper tub at the end of the night.

RUSSIAN AND TURKISH BATHS CAFÉ

An East Village institution

268 East 10th Street, East Village, NY 10009
(212) 674-9250
russianturkishbaths.com
Open 365 days a year
L train/1st Av; 6 train/Astor Pl; N and R trains/8th St – NYU
Inexpensive

There may be no greater social equalizer than the Russian and Turkish Baths in the East Village. In an earlier era, lower Manhattan was dotted with bathhouses where residents from all walks of life would come to steam, cleanse, and revitalize. One of today's last bastions is on 10th Street between 1st Avenue and Avenue A, staying strong and distinctive amidst a rapidly changing neighborhood.

Opened in 1892, the baths have welcomed not only the local community but also celebrities like Mick Jagger, Frank Sinatra, and John F. Kennedy Jr. As reported by the New York Times, legend has it that the Russian "Radiant Room," a veritable inferno of 15 tons of rock cooked overnight, was built from the headstones of cemeteries.

The restaurant at the baths is completely hidden from the street, with nary a window in sight. Stepping inside is not unlike being transported into a Cold War shelter that wasn't notified in 1989. A VCR feeds into two televisions while old newspaper clippings about the spa line the walls. A single worker behind a long deli-like counter serves up classics like Russian borscht soup, Polish sausage, Siberian *pelmeni*, and Baltic herring. Bringing the place incongruously into the 21st century are the American breakfast omelets and smoothie bar, with offerings like Energy Booster and Fantasy Island.

Wine and beer are also available, but if the managers take a liking to you, they just might give you a taste of their own stash of cognac and other spirits. Plastic and styrofoam cups are brought out, food is shared, and a family is born. On your way out, they'll give you hugs and kisses.

The latest owners of the Russian and Turkish Baths are Boris Tuberman and David Schapiro, who bought the baths together in 1985 but operate on different weeks due to a dispute between them going back to 1993. Visiting on a "Boris week" is a completely different experience from visiting on a "David week," both in terms of amenities and clientele. David has opened the baths to Groupon deals while Boris has not; multi-visit passes sold by one owner are not honored by the other. The quirky backstory is told in hot steam rooms by long-time patrons who say they have to keep their calendar organized in order to remember which weeks they can take in the baths.

As you leave, refreshed enough to take on the city that never sleeps, revel in the kitschy wall murals of the Greek and Roman baths and sit on the park bench that is placed in the entranceway of the East Village tenement building. In a few seconds, you'll walk outside down a set of stairs and re-enter the present day, leaving a small, disappearing pocket of New York City.

STREECHA UKRAINIAN KITCHEN

Homemade food by church volunteers

33 East 7th Street, East Village, NY 10003
(212) 674-1615
Friday to Sunday 11am–4pm
6 train/Astor Pl
Inexpensive

Streecha Ukrainian Kitchen is one of those spots that doesn't have to try – either to be known or to be hidden. It's accessed through the basement door of an East Village brownstone that houses a chiropractor's office, located diagonally across from St. George Ukrainian Catholic Church, with which it is affiliated. When it first opened, the only thing that denoted its existence was a piece of laminated paper hanging from a clothes line, with the names of three dishes. Over time, one paper sign became two sheets on the window. Today, there are two vinyl signs, one completely in Ukrainian and the other with the restaurant name on it. Still, it remains nondescript and very easy to miss on a block that has other high-profile destinations like McSorley's Ale House, one of the oldest bars in the city.

Restaurant is a misnomer however, as it has the feel of a church canteen, which it is. But it's open to the public, with operating hours on Friday through Sunday. The menu is small but targeted, offering four main dishes: borscht soup (in cup or bowl), Ukrainian potato dumplings known as *varenyky*, stuffed cabbage with pork and rice called *holobutsi*, and sausage with sauerkraut. The dumplings are hand-rolled starting as early as six in the morning by church volunteers. The proceeds from the kitchen support the church and its private school.

The parish of St. George has been in the neighborhood for over a hundred years and Streecha Ukrainian Kitchen is straight out of the 1970s, when it first opened. The walls are of beige tile and sky blue paint. The tables are covered with polyester tablecloths and the metal folding chairs clang around as visitors rearrange the seats along the long communal tables. Condiments like salt, pepper, mustard, and sugar are displayed in Tupperware boxes, and religious paintings hang on the walls to complete the picture. Despite the dated atmosphere and fluorescent lights, the place buzzes with positive energy during popular hours, just like a get-together at a community organization.

The fare is simple and affordable with the dumplings at $0.75 a piece, the hearty stuffed cabbage at $4.00, and the cup of borscht soup at just $2.00. The coffee is nothing to write home about, but it's just $1.00. There's also an assortment of baked goods like powdered jelly donuts, cinnamon danish, and cheesecake, along with packed Hostess Donettes.

The hours can be unpredictable – the food's available until it runs out, basically – so get here on the earlier side of the afternoon and bring cash.

TIGRE

"Then the door opens"

105 Rivington Street, East Village, NY 10002
(646) 951-2780
tigrenyc.com
Sunday & Monday 5pm–12am, Tuesday & Wednesday 5pm–1am, Thursday to Saturday 5pm–2am

When Tigre's owners gut-renovated the space, they initially planned on replacing the pre-existing, graffiti- and sticker-covered door left behind from the nightclub that previously occupied the address, but ultimately they chose to keep it.

"It's street art. It also creates a little bit of intrigue," said Tigre co-owner Joshua Boissy, noting that it also pays homage to the changing face of the Lower East Side. "Then the door opens."

Inside, the swanky Rivington Street space, opened in November 2023, is far from gritty. The owners sought to create a bar that harkened back to another era of New York, one of disco and Studio 54, Halston and Grace Jones – a "polished steel, microsuede, martini-marbled fantasy" that "evokes the elegance and style of the glamorous age of downtown NYC" as the website puts it.

"We wanted Tigre to be a place that was about escapism, that was sophisticated and refined, but there's also an edge to it," said Boissy, who also co-owns Williamsburg oyster bar Maison Premiere.

They settled on a cocaine-chic aesthetic, with mirrored ceilings, patterned carpets and banquettes covered in a tiger print sourced from a mill in Milan.

The layout includes a U-shaped bar, past which banquettes with copper tables hug the perimeter. It was designed "to see and be seen – everyone's watching each other," said Boissy.

Down the long entry hallway is a single booth tucked behind a chainmail mesh curtain, and then the golden-lit main space. Another room in the back offers privacy and, through a porthole, a view of the bar.

The cocktail menu is divided into categories. There's "then" with the airmail, Rolls Royce and Tahiti club, among others, and "now" – including the mister softee, foreign places, se si bon. There are also sections for coolers, mists, sonics, alcohol-free drinks and martinis,

As for food, there is a smattering of small plate options, including wagyu skewers, tuna tartare and, for $145, 30 grams of Royal Ossetra Caviar paired with house crisps, chive and creme fraiche. And, as with Boissy's other venue, there are also oysters.

SUSHI ON ME

An unexpected subterranean experience

71–26 Roosevelt Avenue (basement), Elmhurst, NY 11372
Text only: (929) 268-5691
instagram.com/sushionme.nyc
Daily from 5pm; final seating at 9:30pm

Omakase has arguably never been as much fun as it is beneath this Jackson Heights–Elmhurst border Chinese food restaurant.

After schlepping out to this less than trendy corner of Queens, you find the entrance to this hot sushi spot in the shadow of the elevated subway, at the bottom of a staircase in front of a takeout joint. The intimate space that awaits has the vague resemblance and layout of a classic sushi bar with a millennial twist. After coming so far, though, it feels rather bizarre – and then the servers start up.

Sushi On Me brings more energy to its omakase servings than many NYC clubs or house parties. Between the unlimited sake and the chefs' antics, the $89 cash-only price tag for the 15-course fishy feast feels more appropriate as an entry fee than the cost of what is functionally dinner and a show. There are flamethrowers, uni shots, raucous singing and other antics galore while, simultaneously, sashimi and nigiri are served piece by piece, their presentation upstaged only by their flavor and freshness.

Early birds may be seated at one of the select few tables, but come dinner time patrons all move up to the long bar. Nights among strangers tend to be the most rowdy, although with only 12 seats it's not hard to fill the whole bar with friends (what's harder is convincing everyone to haul so far out into Queens).

Once the final course is served (unless you're lucky enough to be the final seating of the night), plates are cleared, the bill is paid, and you're expected to hastily make room for the next group. In all, the diversion only lasts about an hour.

The under $100 meal is arguably on par with plenty of far pricier tasting menus throughout the city, yet at a fraction of the cost and exponentially more fun.

Not a fan of journeying nearly to LaGuardia Airport just to enjoy 60 minutes of seafood and energized company? Sushi on Me also opened in Williamsburg, with a $129, 18-course Thai Japanese tasting menu over a span of 90 minutes. The original location, though, surely cannot be beat for an unexpected subterranean experience and high-brow heathen use of a deep Queens basement.

EL SABROSO

Hole in the wall countertops

265 West 37th Street, Garment District, NY 10018
Monday to Friday
7, A, C and E trains/42nd St; 1, 2 and 3 trains/Penn Station
Inexpensive

There are few hidden places that keep their character over time in New York City without succumbing to the trendy crowd, but the hole-in-the-wall restaurants tucked away in Garment District freight entrances were created to cater to manufacturing workers and continue to serve them at cheap prices. Adding to the unique ambience, the doors constantly open and close for deliveries at the active loading docks. But don't expect anything more than a countertop and a few stools – the personal experience at these spots make them worth the adventure.

Self-proclaimed as "the best kept secret in the Garment District," Nick's Place, located on 39th Street, is the most well-known but it's also the least interesting in terms of both cuisine and space. A more hidden option is El Sabroso at 265 West 37th Street.

El Sabroso has been open for over twenty years with the same owner serving affordable Hispanic food. The nondescript sign outside reads "*Aqui ahorra y come bueno*" ("Here you will save and eat well"). Despite a full menu on the wall, your best bet is to ask Tony what he recommends for the day. For $6, you can get the stews that come with a plate of rice, beans, and lettuce. Don't forget to add some of the hot sauce, a secret family recipe Tony won't reveal. Empanadas with cheese or chicken are just $1 each.

There are five stools at the counter and a small wooden table if you want to eat in. Most patrons take out, but if you stay for a chat with Tony he might start to tell you of his trials and tribulations looking for a wife in this city.

An added bonus: the tourists from nearby Times Square rarely venture into this neighborhood and it's a little too far for the Madison Avenue lunch crowd, meaning both the clientele and the restaurants stay true to how they've always been.

DEAR IRVING

A time traveler's fantasy

55 Irving Place, Gramercy, NY 10003
dearirving.com
Monday to Thursday 5pm–2am; Friday to Saturday 5pm–3am; Sunday 5pm–1am
4, 5, 6, L, N, Q and R trains/Union Sq
Moderate

n his film "Midnight in Paris", Woody Allen explores the idea that everyone – no matter when they were born – feels a kinship with a ertain era in the past. Maybe it's just the romantic notion of being ble to look back on a simpler time with rose-colored glasses, which, of ourse, is impossible except in hindsight.

Dear Irving was inspired by that idea – that anyone can feel aligned vith a period in history, and might feel at home if they could immerse hemselves in it. The bar, located in a historic townhouse on Irving Place vhere O. Henry lived, has a time-traveling theme.

Dear Irving comprises four rooms that climb farther and farther nto the past: up front is a '60s-inspired room with midcentury modern urniture, zebra-striped wallpaper, and decorations. Next, there's a 20s-style room, fit for Gatsby and Daisy, with oversized silver armchairs nd crystal curtains. The next room back houses the actual bar, which ontinues with the '20s theme until it abruptly becomes an 1880s hemed room, all red upholstery and pressed-tin ceilings. The final oom is Rococo-themed, like Marie Antoinette's parlor. There are Louis XIV armchairs, white molding with gold trim, an antique mirror, and a uge crystal chandelier. You can find your place and stick to it or wander etween the rooms.

Dear Irving is owned and operated by the team behind Raines Law Room and the Raines Law Room at the William, and the cocktail rogram (presented like a hotel folio) was designed by Meaghan Dorman. You could easily stick to the house drinks, like the Vice Versa gin, grapefruit, bitter, pamplemousse liqueur, and rosé cava), or go vith the bartender's choice.

There's a menu of small plates too, done up in the style of upscale ar food, and inspired by various European traditions: croque monsieur, hicken liver and foie gras parfait, a shrimp cocktail and a cheese plate. A little plate of slow-cooked octopus with almond cream and tomato onfit comes out of the kitchen so perfectly (tender yet firm), it'll hange your mind about octopus forever, and it will make you think wice about your standard barfood choices.

There are desserts too, like the sublime panna cotta, which arrives in a cocktail glass, under a layer of red berry coulis with strawberry garnish. This is definitely a place to come when you want to indulge.

TAPROOM AT THE PLAYERS CLUB

The oldest private club in New York City still in its original location

16 Gramercy Park South, Gramercy, NY 10003
(212) 475-6116
theplayersnyc.org
Open to members: Monday to Friday 5pm–10pm
Many events open to non-members
N, R and 6 trains/23rd St
Moderate

There aren't many places left in New York where you can imbibe whiskey and gin surrounded by artifacts like Mark Twain's pool cue, 19th-century Shakespearean costumes, and portraits by John Singer Sargent. The Players Club, a Greek revival townhouse on Gramercy Park, is one of these places. In fact, it is the oldest private club in New York City still in its original location. Walking into the Players Club feels like stepping back in time to the Gilded Age. Yet because it has always been a private club, few people know about it.

In New York City real-estate terms, the Players Club is enormous – sprawled out over four stories, plus the grill and taproom on the lower level. In the parlor, a large fireplace, antique sofas, tables, and club chairs greet visitors. Upstairs in the card room, guests can see where Mark Twain and Stanford White played poker. The library is full of books and artifacts relating to the theater, including a bust of Edgar Allen Poe and black and white photographs of the actresses who were not allowed to be members (the club was male only until 1989).

Downstairs in the grill and taproom, Mark Twain's pool cue hangs near the pool table. Portraits of the club's famous members (including John Barrymore, Cary Grant, Gregory Peck, Liza Minelli, Ethan Hawke, Kevin Spacey, and Jimmy Fallon) line the walls of the stairwell and the taproom. If you're lucky, you might get a glimpse at the Players Club founder Edwin Booth's bedroom on the third floor. It still smells of the tobacco he smoked incessantly and contains his most cherished objects, including the skull that a fan left to him to use in "Hamlet".

The club's illustrious history began as a result of one of the most turbulent events in American history. After John Wilkes Booth assassinated President Lincoln, his brother Edwin Booth (a great Shakespearean actor) felt he had to do something to remove the stain on the Booth family name. In 1888, he founded the Players Club, a private club where actors (considered rabble rousers at the time) could meet men of society and elevate their status. Fifteen other incorporators joined him, including Mark Twain and William Tecumseh Sherman. Famed architect Stanford White (a club member) redesigned the façade that looks out over Gramercy Park and the statue of Edwin Booth in Shakespearean garb. Club members can use the key that opens the gates to the private park.

The Players Club is open to members Monday through Friday. The club hosts many events, including readings and interactive plays, giving non-members the chance to see this incredible place.

124 OLD RABBIT CLUB

Beer bar with a ’60s rock’n’roll vibe

124 Macdougal Street, Greenwich Village, NY 10012
(212) 254-0575
Daily 6pm–2am
A, B, C, D, E, F and M trains/West 4th St
Inexpensive – cash only

Follow the yellow street art-style rabbit painted onto the external wall of this Greenwich Village beer bar and go down the rabbit hole. Except for that rabbit, the exterior of this place is completely black and nondescript. But head downstairs and into a tiny, cave-like bar for one of the best beer selections in the city.

You might feel like you've stepped into a dingy 1970s watering hole, with rock'n'roll posters taped up on the brick walls, especially if they happen to be playing the Rolling Stones. Though much of Greenwich Village – especially Macdougal Street – has become a victim of its own hipness, the Old Rabbit Club feels like a stalwart reminder of the Village's bohemian roots. Nearby you can still see the bars like Cafe Wha? where Bob Dylan and Jimi Hendrix performed for beatniks and hippies in the '60s, though now they mostly cater to NYU frat boys and tourists. Perhaps because of its secrecy, the Old Rabbit Club feels much more authentic. The only unfortunate relic of times past: it's cash only.

The place is so narrow, there's barely enough room to squeeze behind the people sitting on barstools at the long bar. If you're lucky, you can snag the table in the back, lit by a little chandelier and framed by rich brocaded wallpaper. There are only two other tables, at the front, by the door. Don't expect to lead on a group conversation here. It's loud, and the setup is better suited to a date, especially since you'll be sitting extremely close to the person on the barstool next to you.

It might take a few minutes to scan the page-long menu. The Old Rabbit Club stocks over seventy beers, many imported from Belgium, Holland, Germany, England, and Scotland. There are craft beers by Danish-born Brooklyn-based brewer Evil Twin, sour beers, and Belgian classics like Chimay, Delirium Tremens, and Palm. Even the pickiest beer aficionado will be impressed by the offerings. There's a small selection of wines, too, but you're better off sticking to what this place does best: beer. When in doubt, ask the bartender for a recommendation. If they take a liking to you, they might offer you one on the house. After a few of those beers, don't forget to take a trip to the bathroom to admire a replica of "Manneken-Pis", Brussels' famous statue of a naughty little boy peeing into a fountain.

THE GARRET

Chill spot above Five Guys

296 Bleecker Street, 2nd Floor, Greenwich Village, NY 10014
(212) 675-6157
garretnyc.com
Seven days a week
1 train/Christopher St
Moderate

The Garret is one of those bars where the bartenders are like your bandmates or your awesome guy roommates. Hidden above Five Guys burgers in Greenwich Village, you have to walk to the very back of the fast-food joint and up a wooden staircase. From the outside, you can only spot some chandeliers through the window and a neon sign that says "Soul," simply because the bar has soul, claims one of the bartenders. The actual sign of The Garret sits on the bar itself.

It's the type of spot where you can start day drinking at 2pm on Saturdays, order a can of Tecate and a shot, and bring up burgers and fries from downstairs. But there are also the impressive creative cocktails with names like Seriously Ain't Fancy and Sunken Santa. It has a laid-back cool that you"d find in a dive bar anywhere around the country, with just the right amount of curation in the decor to have personality without pretension. With street art under the fireplace, hilarious photographs, old books and hourglasses scattered around, it manages to please both the trendy cocktail connoisseur and those looking for an easy spot to chill.

The inside of the bathroom door is lined floor to ceiling with 96 gold doorknobs in an almost surrealist work of art, installed by Greenwich Locksmiths. Greenwich Village residents will recognize the nearby locksmith shop, with its façade made entirely of swirling locks.

The wooden chairs and tables could have been pulled straight out of a treehouse, fitting because the space is blessed with two enormous skylights, making it a rare hidden bar with tons of natural light.

For those still looking for exclusive gems, there are Five Guys burgers you can order that aren't available at any other location, like The Garret Burger using Peter Luger sauce, the Italian Neighbors burger with Ottomanelli Bros prosciutto, and the Sixth Man Burger with sriracha.

But most importantly, you'll leave The Garret feeling like you found a bar that feels genuine: both a great place to bring friends or to stop by and chat with the gregarious bartenders. With so many exclusive places in New York City on the cocktail circuit, The Garret is a breath of fresh air.

LITTLE BRANCH

A family affair in a basement bar

20 7th Avenue South, Greenwich Village, NY 10011
(212) 929-4360
Daily 7pm–3am
1 train/Houston St
Moderate

On a bustling block of 7th Avenue, around the corner from the swimming pool with the mural that Keith Haring painted, stands a little flatiron building with a nondescript brown door. On busy nights, there might be a bouncer waiting, but if there isn't, you can get close enough to see a peephole, the likes of which are on many an apartment door in this city. The subtle message seems to be: come drink in my house, but act respectfully, as if you were my guest.

Once in the door, you'll have to descend a long staircase into the basement bar. It's easy to imagine that this is what a true speakeasy would have looked like – not some opulent temple to booze, but somebody's humble basement where hooch was shared with friends the owner knew he could trust. There is certainly a '20s vibe emanating from the place. Look around and you'll notice the pressed tin on the bar, the slightly beat-up brown leather booths, the tables made from safety glass, the corrugated tin ceiling, the vintage cash register with keys like a typewriter's, and the black-and-white family photos and knick-knacks (including many period pieces from that era).

Little Branch is the second bar opened by Sasha Petraske and Joseph Schwartz, who have a hand in several of New York's most renowned cocktail bars, most notably Milk & Honey. And like many Prohibition-era speaks, this is largely a family operation. Joseph manages the bar, his younger brother Ben is the head bartender; and bartender Becky McFalls is married to Joseph's twin brother Louis, who waits on tables. Down in the basement bar, they serve classic cocktails as they were intended to be served, according to precise recipes laid out in books like "The Savoy Cocktail Book", published in 1930 by Harry Craddock, an American who went to London to escape Prohibition and became a renowned barman at the American Bar at The Savoy.

Little Branch was among the first bars to always make cocktails with fresh juices and stock the liquors that they like best, regardless of how expensive or hard-to-get they are. There's a small menu printed with a list of classic cocktails, but you'd be just as well off going with the bartender's choice. They pride themselves on listening to what you like and making something that fits the bill. The beginning of the week is the best time to come, as wait times are shorter, and there's live jazz starting at 10pm.

FREVO

A 16-seat counter behind one of the works in an art gallery

48 W 8th Street, Greenwich Village, NY 10011
frevonyc.com
reservations@frevonyc.com
Tuesday to Saturday for dinner: reservations only

This art gallery is more than it appears. There is little to distinguish Frevo from any other storefront display room, but behind one of the works in its rotating solo exhibitions is the entrance to a C-shaped, 16-seat counter surrounding an open-format kitchen.

"The hidden door behind one of the featured artworks adds to a very New York experience where not all of the city's secrets are made available to the naked eye and you have to be part of the conversation in order to know," says Frevo co-owner Bernardo Silva. The name, he explains, is an interpretation of the word for "to boil" in his native Portuguese, and is meant to reference the fact that the dual restaurant and exhibition space is "not static, but in constant evolution."

Not only does the art change every three months but so does the seasonal menu and wine pairings offered to guests who score spots at one of two nightly counter seatings. For those looking for even more intimacy, there is a single seating every night at Frevo's two tables, together accommodating 10 guests.

The contemporary culinary endeavor claims to reflect "the energy of New York City itself" with its multicultural influences and elegant, refined approach to modern dining, and many critics agree. The restaurant successfully embodies the ease of exclusivity with which some of this town's elite glide through culture, pulling "the ladder up behind them," as Pete Wells writes in the New York Times.

The multicourse tasting menu promises to feed patrons only the finest, most sustainable of bites, all extensively researched by Brazilian chef Franco Sampogna, who takes pride in locating and working with producers whom he deems the best.

The current menu is foie gras-heavy: the ingredient is involved in two courses, one with black truffle and the other with smoked eel.

The Wine Pairing features a boutique-sized selection, including rare vintages and choices from off-the-beaten-path makers. Looking for the most, peak, Premium Wine Pairing? This elevated version costs more than double the entry tier. Many other add-ons, all at additional cost, are available.

Dietary restrictions cannot be accommodated (although, if given sufficient warning, single-ingredient issues can be), parties of one to four must pre-pay, and reservations can only be made through a platform called Tock.

AMERICAN LEGION POST 398

"We're not secretive but we don't advertise our jazz evenings"

248 W 132nd Street, Harlem, NY 10027
(212) 283-9701
Thursday to Sunday, evenings only

Even as other posts of this U.S. veterans' association see membership levels drop, American Legion Post 398 has kept its guest book filled with visitors' names. Significantly, that's because this Harlem branch of the group doesn't just offer assistance to vets but music for all.

Located in the basement of a Harlem brownstone, this saloon is discreet, although a sign balanced atop its parlor windows does announce to the world: "American Legion Col. Charles Young Post #398 and Auxiliary."

"We're not secretive but we don't advertise," says Edward Feaster, the Post's First Vice Commander, a retired social worker and one of multiple Post 398 managers who maintain the space, getting it ready for vets, locals and whoever else might pass by to unwind during open hours.

Post 398's first concerns are to help veterans get their benefits, walk widows through funerary matters and the like, but four nights of the week the headquarters is additionally opened up for a "chance to dance, relax" and "comradeship."

On Thursday, Friday and Saturday nights there's a DJ and on Sunday nights there's jazz. "It's more about providing services than jazz," says Feaster when explaining the club's internal priorities, adding that, despite its reputation, "We're not a jazz bar – we sponsor jazz."

But jazz is what Post 398 is known for. It all started in 1998, when Army vet, musician and Legion regular Seleno Clarke needed somewhere to store his over 400-pound Hammond organ. Clarke, who founded Harlem Groove Band, asked the Legion if his Hammond could stay at the brownstone. He was granted permission, but with the proviso that he play it. And so a tradition was born of Sunday jazz performances.

Although primarily intended for veterans and their guests, all are welcome at Post 398. But everyone has to sign the guest book, and the vibe is mellow and mature. "We call this the post for grown folks. It's not a teenage place," says Feaster. "People can come here, have a good time, sit down and enjoy themselves."

Airplane booze bottles are used for drinks – "It's a lot easier," Feaster explains. And homestyle meals are also available for no more than $12 each from a chef who brings her own Sterno pads to make magic in the stoveless back kitchen. On sunny days, there's a sprawling backyard with its own bar area. Upstairs is for meetings, offices and shooting pool. The walls are filled with military memorabilia and original building details, dusty but untouched.

Although Clarke passed away in 2017, the Hammond still holds court on stage by the entrance.

JAZZ AT MARJORIE ELIOT'S

Jazz shows in a Harlem living room

555 Edgecombe Avenue, 3F, Harlem, NY 10032
(212) 781-6595
Sunday sets start at 2pm, 4pm and 6pm

Whatever the weather, if it's a Sunday afternoon, Marjorie Eliot hosts jazz shows in her Harlem living room. She has been doing this for more than 30 years.

During performances, guests are seated on a bench and folding chairs that spill over from her parlor into her hallway and living room. Wrapped apple cinnamon bars are served and, on a recent Sunday, so were water bottles and apple cider. There is no cover, and the snacks are offered free of charge. (A donation bucket and Venmo handle are available for those who want to say thank you in cash.)

The concerts, at which Eliot often performs herself, have turned her into a local legend. This is not an opinion but a fact: the urban folk culture nonprofit City Lore formally honored her as a living city treasure in 2000. At that point, Eliot's Sunday parlor jazz tradition was less than a decade old. She began it in 1992 as a way to bring joy to a dark day of the week, after her son Phil died due to kidney-related problems at age 32. He passed on a Sunday in 1992.

"I could depend on it like clockwork, to feel bad on Sunday," she told the New York Daily News in 2009. Opening her home and offering uplifting entertainment to others helped soothe her broken heart. When "people come here to be my guests, they make a sad story into something joyous," she said.

Despite her generosity and hospitality, Eliot – an actress and pianist who, over the years, successfully eluded having her age printed in numerous media write-ups – finds the concerts so fulfilling, she believes that "I get more than I give."

When another of her sons, Shawn Eliot, disappeared in 2011, the concerts continued. That Sunday, she handed out fliers with his picture to her guests.

Many have graced her home stage over the years, and former regulars and performers in town for the weekend, or stopping by after a time away, will often be pulled up from the crowd to join Marjorie in song. The musical roster generally includes a mix of jazz, pop and spirituals.

Her neighbors at the landmarked Paul Robeson Residence, named for the late actor and resident after he died in 1976, have never much minded the weekly transformation of the third-floor apartment into a music venue.

The strength of this one woman's generosity and spirit alone has kept alive an unconventional performance space which has now outlasted countless other establishments to become, truly, a New York institution.

One time, when the police came in response to a noise complaint, they stayed to listen, the New York Times reported in 2003.

CHEZ ZOU

A concealed cocktail cantina just as posh as its name

Suite 85, 385 9th Avenue, Hudson Yards, NY 10001
(212) 380-8585
chezzou.com
Sunday 2pm–midnight; Monday 5pm–midnight; Tuesday to Friday 5pm–1am; Saturday 2pm–1am

Situated in the developer-built neighborhood of Manhattan West (the neighboring corporate mixed-use project to the better-known Hudson Yards), those in the know access this watering hole through the downstairs restaurant which bears half its name twice.

To get to Chez Zou, patrons first enter Zou Zou's, then locate the host stand, enter the elevator behind it, and ride up to the fourth floor. Once there, an impeccably designed space awaits with uniquely patterned black-and-white flooring, curving benches and tastefully mirrored ceiling lights. Large leafy plants abound. A patio offers shaded turquoise and pink seats beneath striped umbrellas, more fronds, and the shadow of many glassy behemoths towering overhead.

Former The NoMad head bartender Joey Smith is shared as beverage director at both Chez Zou and Zou Zou's. Smith, who spent years learning modernist techniques from the "godfather of modernist cocktails, Dave Arnold" at the bar Booker and Dax, has applied that knowledge to Chez Zou's menu, where drinks incorporate traditional flavors of the Levant region as well as "staples of the New York cocktail haunt," says Smith.

"A cocktail at Chez Zou should simultaneously transport you worlds away while still making you feel right at home," poeticizes Smith, offering a cinematically dramatic description more akin to the synopsis for a romantic thriller than a new above-restaurant bar. "When last call is done, and you enter the bright streets of a Manhattan night, your experience in Chez Zou should linger like a good dream. The difference is you can relive this dream any evening you're on the West Side."

In presentation, this looks like drinks combining "bourbon and banana, mezcal and clove, white rum and dill, and more." There's also a Mediterranean-inspired menu of appetizers and shareable offerings, although far less extensive than the one on the next floor down.

Below, at the high-ceilinged, 75-seat Zou Zou's, the open kitchen is centered around a wood-fired hearth and produces a robust menu of modern Eastern Mediterranean food, with cuisine inspiration credit due to Lebanon, Israel, Turkey, Egypt, Syria and Jordan "among others." There's more bread options than some bars have beer – grilled *bazlama* (a Turkish village bread), fresh-baked *talami* (a Lebanese focaccia) and honey-butter *kubaneh* (a Yemeni pull-apart roll), to name a few.

As for the architecture at this bright and colorful, socialite-friendly hot spot, there are arches galore, blue and green tiles cover the floor and domes abound.

© Alix Piorun

THE 1850 SPEAKEASY

A bar within a lounge within an airport

Terminal 4 (level 4), JFK Airport, Queens, NY 11430
thecenturionlounge.com/locations/jfk
Daily 5am–10pm

This exclusive spot may feature the same recycled air as the rest o John F. Kennedy International Airport, but it's a welcome repriev in the eye of a bustling storm.

Open to American Express card members only, the Centurio Lounge at JFK offers a little bit of cordoned-off respite for wear travelers either starting or going home from their journeys. Located pas TSA – and thus inaccessible to anyone who isn't genuinely traveling – i the sprawling airport's Terminal 4, the Lounge is located just beyond th security checkpoint to the left of the escalators leading to the gate level

Inside, the Lounge is surprisingly spacious, especially when compare to an aircraft: it has two full bars and one speakeasy-style space sprea across more than 15,000 square feet. There's a two-floor guest lounge a spa and wellness space from Equinox (intended specifically for th experience of preparing to fly), six rooms each themed to a differen New York City landmark or era and, tucked beyond one copper-panele wall, The 1850 Speakeasy.

Named for the year of American Express' founding, The 1850 is neant to evoke the Prohibition era as well as "New York's style, history nd glam," says American Express global lounge experiences general nanager Pablo Rivera.

The JFK Lounge, he notes, is the largest in AmEx's network of airport elaxation stations. In contrast, other airport lounges all look extremely imilar, cookie-cutter corporate attempts at making the hell that is nodern air travel slightly more palatable. Only, beyond the smaller ootprints of the other lounges, lesser cities than New York await.

Hungry? Four-time James Beard Award nominee chef Ignacio Mattos created the lounge's menu, which includes wild mushroom farro isotto, *brasato al Barolo* and buttermilk pancakes with caramelized pple, vanilla and cardamom.

The sprawling in-airport sanitarium also offers amenities such as rge flat-screen TVs, a phone room, a family room, a member services esk, workspaces and high-speed WiFi.

For those whose flight schedule and credit-card holdings align and llow them entry, the Lounge is certainly worth a visit. Although its otel-like furnishings and atmosphere hardly transport patrons outside f JFK, the meta nature of drinking at a bar within a lounge within an irport certainly makes for a more memorable pre-flight experience than nything that can be found in the main terminal.

© Alix Piorun

© Alix Piorun

J. BESPOKE

An exclusive hideaway for sports fans accessed through an unmarked door in the back of a coffee shop

121 E 27th Street, Kips Bay, NY 10016
(212) 213-2931
jbespoke.com
Monday to Saturday 5pm "till late"; Sunday closed

Sports bar, but make it bougie: that's the concept behind J. Bespoke, an upscale, 50-seat lounge "with a focus on sports programming" accessed through a café. There are no associated teams, the seats at the bar aren't stools, and spilling beer on anything would be quite the faux pas. Besides, the emphasis isn't on the beer but the $18 on-tap cocktails.

"The property is an exclusive hideaway for sports fans and their cohort seeking an elevated cocktail experience," in the words of the co-founders, brothers Jesse and Eric Jacobs. The pair believe they've found an "untapped niche": a space for sports fans who want to watch the game not in large, impassioned groups but amid upholstered banquettes and carefully appointed armless armchairs in a conference-room-like hermitage with the word "bespoke" in its title.

Most games are muted; an exception is made for Super Bowl-echelon events (which are projected on a special screen, unlike the rest), the announcers replaced with a musical soundtrack kept at a volume that still allows guests to make conversation. And when the game is done, the TVs are "hidden away" or made to show digital art so the "cocktails, bites and music take center stage."

J. Bespoke's takes on plebeian favorites include not pub cheese but a $22 charcuterie board and no peanuts but, yes, spiced nuts. While there are wings, they cost $16 and involve *oregenata*. There are also fries – waffle fries, with "fine sea salt," for $9.

The Jacobs brothers believe they're pioneers in the freshly identified market of sophisticated sports lovers looking to watch their team play in a velvet-filled, brass-accented back room accessed through an unmarked door in the back of a coffee shop. Gone is the sticky bar, the home team jerseys on the walls, the beer-shot specials – at J. Bespoke, the bar is slick, the walls are covered in art and wood panels, and the front-facing Colombian coffee business, Devoción, is known for its coffee cherry tea or *cascara* bar.

After so many years being disappointed by innumerable sports bars that were too rowdy, too loud, too basic in their menu offerings and overall a disappointment, the brothers have at last created their ideal sports program-viewing paradise.

EDIE'S

A hidden bar within a bar, behind the large painted lips on a rear wall

380 3rd Avenue, Kips Bay, NY 10016
(212) 686-6380
thefactory380.com
Only open for private events

At this Andy Warhol-themed watering hole in Kips Bay, there's a hidden Easter egg only those in-the-know will come upon. A secret room named Edie's in the back of the main space serves as a reference within a reference and a bar within a bar. This secondary taproom, named for the late fashion model and Warhol muse Edie Sedgwick, is located behind the large painted lips on a rear wall, and is only revealed to those who ask what lies past (really, it's not too hard to find).

Those granted access enter through a black steel door at the end of a narrow hallway, "Nothing to see here" written in hot pink spray paint on its wall. Once inside, the much smaller, mirrored and metallic-painted area offers its own under-lit bar, marble-topped tables and bitty chandelier in the center of the sloped ceiling – a slightly quieter offshoot of the large, often boisterous main space full of a predictable Kips Bay crowd. As well, there's a full-wall mural created by graffiti artist Jules Muck of Sedgewick. One of Warhol's superstars and a lasting style icon, the "it girl" of the 1960s tragically passed away of an overdose at 28 in 1971.

Further Warhol callbacks are peppered through the 2,700-square-foot front, including a curated collection of photos from Studio 54, where Warhol was a frequent visitor, among other favorite nightlife locations of his, as well as self-portraits. Red-cushioned wooden benches, a leopard-print rug, a neon sign reading "I Wish I Could Paint Our Love" and a disco ball add further flair. "But I Always Say, One's Company, Two's A Crowd, And Three's A Party," a proverb of Warhol's, reads a pink-painted wall.

And, of course, the bar's name is a nod to Warhol's infamous studio, The Factory. In addition to the full bar and menu of $14 "factorytails" (among them, the gin and St-Germain-based "Camera Adds 10 Lbs" and the pineapple-infused, tequila-focused "You're On Mute") there's a full food menu heaping with classic diner food and bar bites as well as some twists, including a peach habanero bacon and burrata B.L.T. and a cookie dough lava cake, the only dessert option.

"The space evokes the spirit and vibe of the Warhol era," says co-owner Scott Connolly, who spent nearly eight years attempting to make his vision for the bar – one shared by his friend and co-owner, Cillian Fanning – a reality. Their execution of the homage has proved a success. Certainly, it has lasted for much longer than 15 minutes of (at least local) fame.

BAR CALICO

An easy-to-miss Southwestern-themed space

23 Lexington Avenue (second floor), Kips Bay, NY 10010
barcaliconyc.com
managers@georgiaroomnyc.com
Monday to Thursday 5pm–11pm; Friday & Saturday 5pm–1am

No exterior signage informs passersby that this Flatiron District hotel is home to Bar Calico, and even once inside, the dimly lit Southwestern-themed space is easy to miss.

Created by Matt Kliegman and Carlos Quirarte, the team behind the celebrity-beloved Ray's and Pete Davidson-invested Pebble Bar, this candlelit watering hole is located down a dark hallway on the Freehand Hotel's second floor. The decor was inspired by mother of American modernism Georgia O'Keeffe and Ghost Ranch, the New Mexico abode which served as the late great painter's home and studio.

With the pair in mind, head bartender Mike Campbell developed Calico's desert-based cocktail menu, focusing on creating "arid" drinks with "unapologetic flavors." The bar's name comes from O'Keeffe's 1931 work, "Cow's Skull with Calico Roses".

The 900-square-foot lounge, located on the Freehand's eastside, underwent a history-focused renovation ahead of its 2021 opening. Its original travertine floors, crown moldings and millwork were restored to appear as they did when the former George Washington Hotel was built in 1930. Surrounding a patinated 10-seat bar sourced from a Prohibition-era Chicago speakeasy are natural textiles and atmospheric lighting meant to give the energy of an artist's living room.

Looking to get a second round elsewhere? At the Freehand, it's possible to bar hop without going outside, what with multiple bars and restaurants conveniently located less than a stone's throw away from each other.

Across the floor, the more recently opened Georgia Room has similar inspirations to Calico but is intended to exude a more animated energy, with room for dancing and an avant-garde disco ball hanging from the ceiling. The two bars are connected by a space called the Studio, which hosts its own roster of events.

Elsewhere in the hotel are the Smile To Go Cafe, the Comodo Restaurant and the Broken Shaker bar. On the ground floor, The Comodo, a new incarnation of former West Village restaurant Comodo, offers up natural wines and Latin American food, and the Broken Shaker (with locations also in Los Angeles, Miami and Chicago) slings drinks and its own menu of bites to anyone who ventures up to the hotel's roof.

GAONNURI

Korean atop an office building with amazing view

1250 Broadway, 39th Floor, Koreatown, NY 10011
(212) 971-9045
gaonnurinyc.com
Seven days a week for dinner, Monday to Friday for lunch
B, D, F, M, N, Q and R trains/Herald Sq or 34th St
Moderate to expensive

There is such a density of restaurants in Koreatown on 33rd Street near Herald Square that there has to be a good reason to visit one of the most upscale on the block.

On the 39th floor, the top level of a nondescript office building at 1250 Broadway, Gaonnuri offers an amazing panorama of the city: a 180 degree view of midtown Manhattan – from the Hudson River looking onto Jersey City to Herald Square and Bryant Park, and the MetLife Building atop Grand Central Terminal. In one corner, you'll find yourself nearly face to face with the Empire State Building.

The restaurant is spacious, with two sets of tall horizontal windows wrapping it. The decor is almost theatrical, stepping down into a semi-circular seating area. The tables by the windows are also equipped with barbeque capability, though the design is so sleek you wouldn't necessarily notice it when the grill is covered.

You can tell Gaonnuri thinks pretty highly of itself, starting with the decor and the dress code. "Please dress appropriately," the sign says, with a list of clothing guests should "refrain from wearing," like sports caps, baggy or ripped jeans, tank tops, flip flops or sneakers.

Go during lunch for the best deal. The lunch *bansang* offers *bulgogi* (traditional marinated sliced beef rib-eye) for $20 or *kalbi* (marinated beef short-rib) for $25. Both come on a wooden tray with rice, soup, and individual side dishes, known as *banchan*. The banchan are refillable, and in addition to the classics like kimchi and spinach, there are some that are not commonly offered at the other Korean restaurants down the street, such as a dish of pickled bellflower with cucumber and squid. The bulgolgi bansang comes on a bed of onion and scallion, with a slice of pumpkin.

The barbeque lunch starts at $23 for chicken and $25 for bulgolgi and sliced pork belly. Other classics like *mandoo* appetizer (steamed dumplings), *japchae* (stir-fried glass noodles), *galbi tang* (short-rib soup), *kimchi jiggae* (spicy kimchi soup with pork and vegetables) and *bibimbap* (rice mixed table side in a hot stone bowl with meat, seafood, or vegetables) are also on the menu. And not surprisingly, as this is both a tourist and business lunch destination, there's an extensive drink menu of hard liquor, wine, and cocktails. Long story short: the food is decent, but the view is better.

THE BACK ROOM

Meyer Lansky and Lucky Luciano's Prohibition speakeasy

102 Norfolk Street, Lower East Side, NY 10002
(212) 228-5098
backroomnyc.com
Sunday and Monday 7:30pm–2am; Tuesday to Thursday 7:30pm–3am; Friday and Saturday 7:30pm–4am
Live jazz on Monday nights
F, J, M and Z trains/Essex St or Delancey St
Moderate

Imagine this: your guide turns the corner, leading you off busy Rivington Street, where the bars have neon signs, and onto a quiet side street. You almost reach the end when she opens a small metal gate with the words "Lower East Side Toy Company" in block letters, and leads you downstairs to a dark, dingy alley. There's no one else around. Just when you start to wonder if she's going to knife you, she leads you up another set of stairs, where a bouncer asks for a password, and opens a door onto another era. There are gold-framed paintings on red damask wallpaper, a mahogany bar backed by mirrors, antique cut-glass chandeliers, Victorian velvet sofas, and marble coffee tables. People are drinking cocktails in teacups and beers in paper bags. Jazz wafts through the air and the room buzzes with energy.

This is not just another period recreation: this was Meyer Lansky's spot. He and Lucky Luciano (two of New York's most notorious Prohibition-era gangsters) used to come here to conduct "business meetings" with the likes of Bugsy Siegel and Frank "the prime minister" Costello. When the current owners, Johnny Barounis and Steven Yee, started working on the space, they discovered a trapdoor in the restaurant upstairs. During Prohibition, gangsters and bootleggers would drop down into the basement, which had escape routes onto Norfolk, Suffolk, and Delancey Streets, in case the cops showed up.

"Back then, the booze was stronger, so they mashed up fruit, added syrups, anything to mask the flavor of the grain alcohol. Whoever had the sweetest drinks had the best cocktail menu," Yee explains. Today, The Back Room serves classics like the French 75 and the Sazerac in teacups – a throwback to those days when revelers tried to conceal their hooch.

The space has operated continuously as a bar since its speakeasy days, but that doesn't mean it always looked so breathtaking. When Barounis and Yee came in, they spent about eight months restoring the bar to its original beauty. They tore down the wallboard to expose the brick underneath, uncovered the wood floors, built it up again, and found antiques to decorate it. "We wanted it to be a speakeasy," Yee says, "but there's more to that than just a hidden entrance. The difference is always going to be how you run your house." That means they won't tolerate any crap from troublemakers. The entrances are guarded, just like they were in Lansky's day, and only a lucky few will ever make it into The Back Room's hidden back room. Even if you find the bookcase on hinges, that doesn't mean you'll make it past the threshold.

The Back Room is nice any night, but on Monday nights, live jazz animates the space. The band starts playing at 9pm, and people start swing dancing around 10.

BEAUTY & ESSEX

Swanky nightclub behind a pawn shop

146 Essex Street, Lower East Side, NY 10002
(212) 614-0146 – beautyandessex.com
Daily 5pm–1am; Saturday and Sunday brunch 11:30am–3pm
F, J, M and Z trains/Delancey St or Essex St
Moderate to expensive

Make no mistake: Beauty & Essex is not for everyone. You don't have to be Jay-Z or Madonna to get in (though they have been known

to party here), but show up underdressed and you won't make it past the pawn shop that serves as a front for the luxe nightclub. The retro, mint-green shop up front is clearly a gimmick, but at least it's a fun one. Managing partner Jared Boles says this place has "the keyhole effect," and it's true – it seems small from the outside, but as you continue to work your way in, it gets bigger and bigger, and more and more luxurious.

For over a century, this building had been M. Katz, a furniture store down the street from Essex Street Market, and seeing the club's vast rooms with soaring ceilings, you can almost imagine what that might have been like. When the principals of the Tao Group (the power players behind twenty restaurants, bars, and clubs in New York and Las Vegas) got their hands on the 10,000 square foot space, they completely gutted it and rebuilt from the ground up. Now the place oozes a very theatrical kind of luxury, giving off a retro glam vibe, like the kind of restaurant where Don Draper and Roger Sterling would bring out-of-town clients who wanted to misbehave.

The group took vintage jewelry as their inspiration, spreading the motif throughout the four dining rooms and lounges. An antique brooch inspired an oversized gold floral wall piece on the ground floor. Upstairs, interlocking antiqued mirrors have the shape of one of the partner's mother's bracelet. The Locket Room (the upstairs dining room) features gilded frames that display lockets instead of paintings. (The staff like to put funny photos and images in them – open them up and you'll see.) A pearl chandelier anchors the Pearl Lounge, where the DJ spins and people dance until the wee hours. But the pièce de resistance is the long crystal chandelier that hangs above the grand staircase.

The jewelry theme extends to the menu as well, where drinks have names like the Emerald Gimlet (muddled basil with vodka, lime, and simple syrup) and Earl the Pearl. There's an extensive list of multiethnic share plates, including a whole section of "jewels on toast," like avocado with lemon and espelette on brioche. Star Chef Chris Santos of the Stanton Social is behind the menu, and took every opportunity to play with witty puns and flavor combinations, like the tuna poke wonton tacos – two-bite crispy wonton shells shaped like tacos wrapped around tuna tartar topped with micro cilantro, radish, and wasabi kewpie. The execution of the food is better than you might expect from a nightclub that probably generates much of its revenue from bottle service.

As you'd expect from the name, the place is full of beautiful people – models, actresses, and women that simply look like models and actresses, plus of course the moguls (one patron reportedly racked up a whopping $45,000 tab and left a $15,000 tip). If the ladies take a long time freshening up, it's because the ladies' lounge downstairs gives away complimentary pink champagne – not that they need it.

FIG. 19

15

Behind an art gallery

131½ Chrystie Street, Lower East Side, NY 10002
info@figurenineteen.com
figurenineteen.com
Tuesday to Saturday 8pm–4am; Sunday 6pm–2am
B and D trains/Grand St; J and Z trains/Bowery
Moderate

To get to Fig. 19 – short for Figure 19 (as if an illustration from a science book) – you have to walk through The Lodge Gallery above the popular subterranean dance spot Home Sweet Home and open up the door in the very back. Once you're inside, it feels like home. In fact, Fig. 19 was created by the owners of Home Sweet Home as a clubhouse for them and the staff to hang out. Originally just an unfinished storage room, they thought, "This could be something better." Home Sweet Home has been a Lower East Side fixture since 2006 and Fig. 19 opened in 2011, a refined update to the woodsy, taxidermy decor of the bar below. First it was just for friends and family, utilizing a membership card system, but now it's open to anyone who knows how to find it.

Everything inside is decorated with the warmth and coziness of a New York City apartment parlor, with the building's original wood plank floor and exposed brick wall. The vintage wooden bar, replete with custom-made animal vertebrae taps, is surrounded by simple stools, while scented candles are scattered throughout the space. Tufted couches built into the wall abut a fireplace fitted with candles and topped with a stuffed peacock. Long, beaded chandeliers hang from the ceiling, including one above a reclaimed wooden table in the back – a great, cozy spot for groups. Friends of the owners curate the art that rotates through the space and a large custom cabinet at the entrance showcases obscura like stuffed birds, skulls, and animal hoof candles. There's also an impressive female bust made of wax whose "tears" were formed when the staff decided to burn the candle.

If you happen to look up, you'll notice that industrial pipes are still exposed and the ceiling is unfinished. Such is the nature of Fig. 19, which has managed to keep away the sceney crowds of New York City by remaining chill and true to its roots. The music that spins in the bar is urban Americana, reminiscent of the sounds that emerged from the indie music scene in Brooklyn in the early 2000s, with references to earlier bands from the '80s like Depeche Mode.

The artisanal cocktails made at Fig. 19 are a tasteful riff on classic cocktails, changing just slightly with the season. The menu was created by the bartender at the Hotel Delmano in Williamsburg, with fun names like Rose Sélavy and Midnight in Paris. There's prosecco on tap (in addition to beers) and a long list of spirits.

There's usually a bouncer in front of the gallery, but don't worry. Say you're headed to Fig. 19, wave to those working in The Lodge Gallery and make your way to the back door.

BLIND BARBER

A barbershop in operation that conceals a dance hotspot

339 East 10th Street, Lower East Side, NY 10009
(212) 228-2123
blindbarber.com
Backroom: Monday to Saturday 6pm–4am
Barbershop: 12pm–9pm (Sundays to 6pm)
L train/1st Av
Moderate

Alphabet City was the first location of Blind Barber, which opened in 2010 and has since expanded to Williamsburg and Los Angeles. Reinventing a popular dance spot in the same location, the entrance to Blind Barber is a two-seat barbershop that is actually in operation. Designed to feel like a retro dentist office, even the barber tools are on rolling dental trays. The entrance to the back-room bar is hidden behind a rolling door, which opens up to a large lounge. The name of the bar is a reference to the names given to speakeasies during Prohibition like Blind Tiger and Blind Pig, a message to policemen to turn a blind eye to the activities going on behind the scenes.

In actuality, the style of the Blind Barber back room is a little more quirky than the term "Prohibition" encompasses, designed by Emporium Designs with some personal touches from the owners. One was obsessed with including an abacus, so there's one built into an overhang above the dance floor. Each owner put framed photographs of their grandparents on the walls, but most have been stolen by inebriated customers by now. There's an eclectic mix of tables ranging from vintage chests to shabby-chic finds, even ones converted from barrels. Don't miss the library parlor room in the back past the bathrooms – it's a cozy escape the owners refer to as "Grandpa's Den."

The cocktail menu has a core selection of house classics, like Strawberry Fields with vodka, lemon juice, honey, strawberries and parsley, and the Smoke + Dagger of whiskey, jalapeño-infused Combier, lemon juice, cucumber, and ginger. The seasonal cocktails change in fall and spring, and pizza is provided until 10 at night by Gnocco next door. Happy hours run from a generous 6pm to 9pm every day the back bar is open. Evenings get busy – expect the dance floor to be packed.

Back to the barber shop, the small room takes advantage of the original exposed brick of the building. Added to the decor are distressed metal boards, vintage Koker barbershop chairs, and wooden auditorium seats. An old barber-shop sterilizer now functions as a side table. The underlying concept is about camaraderie, a nod to the barbershops of yore where a community would come together. To that end, Blind Barber offers a drink with your shave – anything from spirits to beer. Just no cocktails until the bar opens at 6pm.

BANZARBAR

A bar above a bar at an alley's end

2 Freeman Alley (upstairs), Lower East Side, 10002
(212) 420-0012
banzarbar.com
Sunday and Monday 6pm–10:30pm; Tuesday to Thursday 6pm–11:30pm; Friday and Saturday 6pm–12:30am

Just a block from Bowery, there's a crack in the street grid called Freeman Alley. A little rivulet of sidewalk off Rivington, the street is a world apart, a calm within the storm of the Lower East Side – albeit one papered in layers of wheat paste and caked in spray paint.

The svelte stretch is so covered in graffiti that it serves as something of an outdoor gallery. At the end of this informal art walk are hung warm bulbs of light, and below them is a restaurant named Freemans. Upstairs, on the second floor at Freemans, there is Banzarbar.

"The space previously was storage and a service bar. The staff always liked to hang out back there and it was cozy, so we expanded on that and built out an intimate private bar," Freemans' founder William Tigertt tells the publication Cool Hunting of the 20-seat room. Its theme was inspired by explorers, its name a reflection of the 1929–31 British Australian New Zealand Antarctic Research Expedition, better known by its abbreviation, BANZARE.

The room was reimagined to look like a ship – an intimate ship because of the restrictive square footage. The exploratory cocktail menu pulls from different global regions, including the Asian spice trade, the alpine herbs of Scandinavia's fjords and East Indies' rums.

Carefully selected dishware includes earthenware cups, Dutch blue and white ceramic cups, vintage egg cups and etched glassware inspired by 18th-century cut crystal. For food, the team went with nautical, and thus the menu has a seafood emphasis. The current lineup includes roasted oysters with kimchi shrimp butter, scallop and shrimp crudo and a whole, wild Portuguese octopus, tempura fried with dill pickles, citrus crema and mustard seeds.

Meanwhile, downstairs, Freemans has been serving up healthy but hearty fare between its taxidermy-covered walls since 2004, when Tigertt came upon the space while scouting for a Halloween party spot. The party never happened, but the restaurant opened the following fall. On this level of the building, the theme is not the tundra but early American tavern, old world tradition, simplicity and rusticness and the bar menu is heavy on American bourbon and rye.

RPM UNDERGROUND

Have a drink under a record shop

54th Street, Midtown, NY 10019
Text only: (914) 439-5065
rpmunderground.us
Daily 1pm–4am

In the bowels of this Midtown record shop, a cavernous space not only slings drinks but also hosts karaoke. A combination event space and vinyl shop, RPM Underground offers old recordings upstairs and the opportunity to make brand new ones below.

On the first floor, an aboveground record shop has 30,000 vinyls for sale. Downstairs, there are two full-service bars, a menu of classic pub grub and 18 private pop-culture-themed rooms for singing karaoke. These include the Slutever Room, an Avengers-themed space, a pinball-themed room and a diner-themed room, the largest of which is capable of hosting parties up to 40. There's also a central area for singing karaoke alongside the general population.

The rather meta menu includes cocktails inspired by the karaoke rooms, including a Jukebox Hero (Stoli vanilla, Lazzaroni maraschino, Coca-Cola), Tangled Up In Booze (involving blue curaçao), and the Thor: Ragna-Rocks (more blue curaçao). There are also draft beer offerings, comfort food, a karaoke brunch special on weekends and bottle service.

On Fridays, drink discounts are available to anyone who dresses according to the theme. Various open mics and comedy shows also dot RPM's calendar.

Upstairs, downstairs and in the connecting staircase and hallway, an art gallery-worth of artifacts, signs and audio equipment hang on the walls – all handpicked from RPM Underground partner Sam Huh's private collection.

"It's really a labor of love," says Raj Banik, another RPM partner, of Huh's extensive accumulation of various commercial-sized decor pieces. The enthusiast has been amassing his quirky empire of collectibles for three decades, sourcing them from flea markets, antique shops, estate sales and the like.

Think the amount of retro industry signage (some of it dating back to the 19th century) on display at RPM is impressive? "Huh has a warehouse full of this stuff, lined wall-to-wall and floor to ceiling," says Banik. In fact, it was the collection itself that significantly inspired the creation of RPM, as Huh wanted a way to show it off. The combination of karaoke and record shop gave him a way to do this, and the vinyl stocked upstairs also comes from his own immense musical assemblage.

Overall, the 11,000-square-foot space succeeds in paying homage to the days when records and radio ruled the airwaves (without being cheesy or overly nostalgic) while also providing a windowless space to lose track of time singing songs while business as usual continues just overhead. Any emotional upset caused by being near Times Square not immediately left at the door tends to quickly dissipate.

DEAR IRVING ON HUDSON

A respected bar in an unexpected, high-up location

310 W 40th Street (40th & 41st floor), Midtown, NY 10018
(917) 261-6908
dearirving.com
Monday to Thursday 5pm–midnight; Friday 5pm–2am; Saturday 4pm–2am; Sunday 4pm–midnight

This open-air hotel bar and lounge claims to be the highest in Manhattan. Way above Midtown, on the 40th and 41st floors of W 40th Street's Aliz Hotel Times Square, this rooftop venue promises to elevate guests' evenings in more ways than one. Not only does Dear Irving on Hudson offer panoramic views from its sky-high setting, but it also has a sommelier-selected wine menu and small plates – an airy reprieve from the rat race below.

The extensive cocktail list is thematically organized into classics, earthier mixes, spicy options, alcohol-free refreshers and local inspirations, including a gin and tonic featuring New York Distilling Company's Dorothy Parker gin, a highball with Writers' Tears Irish whiskey and the Pullin' Me Back In with ragtime rye, honey, amaro sfumato and both angostura and mole bitters (all $19 each). Seasonal additions are also rotated in and out.

Nosh choices include filet mignon bites, petite abeille sliders with wagyu beef, and wild mushroom croquettes served with truffle garlic aioli.

Like Dear Irving Gramercy, its older, same-name sister bar, the dual-level space has been decorated in accordance with a loose time-travel theme. The lower floor has been given Art Deco accents and the upper is intended to look like the set of a 1960s James Bond film, concealed areas included.

The space features four balconies, but most of the square footage is indoors. The team behind Dear Irving on Hudson has thus angled away from calling it a rooftop bar as really, they feel, it's more of a penthouse. "We're definitely trying to stay away from rooftop and that connotation, because most of the real estate is inside," bar director and owner Meaghan Dorman (who curates the menus at both Dear Irving locations) told Eater shortly ahead of the Midtown location's opening in January 2019. "We've been calling it 'Dear Irving with a view' amongst ourselves."

The first Dear Irving, aptly located on Irving Place, opened in 2014, and has earned itself a reputation as one of the city's most revered cocktail bars in the years since. At the original Gramercy spot, the space is divided into four rooms, each themed for a different historic figure: there's a Marie Antoinette room, an Abraham Lincoln room, a JFK room and an F. Scott Fitzgerald room. The uniting concept is Woody Allen's 2011 film, "Midnight in Paris".

Although it doesn't offer the same sweeping views as its sister establishment, it does boast hand-carved ice and buzzer-equipped tables to ensure the most high-quality service.

NOTHING REALLY MATTERS

Harried commuters routinely stop in after missing a train, only to stay so long they miss another

Inside the downtown 1 station at W 50th Street, Midtown, NY 10019
instagram.com/nothingreallymattersbar
Monday to Saturday 4pm–2am; closed Sunday

It's difficult to imagine a more perfect address for such a nihilistically named watering hole. In a filthy corner of a Midtown subway station, past the glowing green light of a digital art gallery and down the crud-caked corridor, a surprisingly high-end saloon lies in wait. Nothing Really Matters took up shop in the 50th Street downtown 1 train entrance on December 31, 2021. Longtime city denizens will recall that its sleek, black-tabled space was once the notorious Siberia Bar, a legendary dive beloved for being a celebrity-ridden den of alcohol-fueled, subterranean chaos. Part of the reason why owner Adrien Gallo decided to go upscale with Nothing Really Matters is in response to this long-gone saloon. He wasn't looking to compete with its infamous, inebriated antics and instead decided to do something entirely different, something that contrasted sharply with the grimy underground world just beyond his front door. And it appears to be working …

"People are really excited, they're like, 'Holy s–t, what's going on down here?'", Gallo tells the New York Post. When the gallery has its screens illuminated, "It throws a really nice glow down the corridor, and you can kind of hear the music faintly from outside my bar – people will walk by and then they walk back. If we see that person more than once, usually by the second or third time, they just come in for a cocktail."

Sometimes harried commuters stop in after missing a train, only to stay so long they miss another. Gallo has also found a clientele among workers grateful for a bar offering up booze till 2am in a neighborhood where such a thing is surprisingly hard to find. Law enforcement and local business initiatives are also grateful for Gallo's presence in the space, he says. Having a lively bar in the desolate hallway beneath Times Square makes it feel exponentially safer, everyone agrees.

Although Gallo was initially alone in the corridor, no longer: after finding success with his unique little cubbyhole, he passed along his landlord's contact info to the pair of DIY world event producers who proceeded to open the gallery next door, slightly further up the stairs towards Midtown beyond.

In recent years, Gallo has expanded his underground empire to include Tiny Dancer, a bitty coffee shop, and See No Evil Pizza, a sit-down restaurant, both directly adjacent to Nothing Really Matters.

© Alix Piorun

CAMPBELL APARTMENT

One of the most magnificent rooms in the entire city, within Grand Central

15 Vanderbilt Avenue, Midtown East, NY 10017
(212) 953-0409
hospitalityholdings.com
Monday to Thursday 12pm–1am; Friday and Saturday 12pm–2am;
Sunday 12pm–midnight
4, 5, 6 and 7 trains/Grand Central
Moderate to expensive

Of all the hidden bars in New York City, the Campbell Apartment is the grandest and most elegant. Yet of the 750,000 people who pass through Grand Central Terminal every day, only a fraction knows it exists. The next time you want to impress someone, lead them to the gilded elevator in the south-west wing of the terminal, below Commodore Vanderbilt's enormous gold light fixtures lined with Edison bulbs, and take them downstairs to the basement. There, up a small set of stairs, you'll find one of the most magnificent rooms in the entire city.

To fully appreciate the Campbell Apartment, you need to know its history. In 1864, industrialization was beginning to dramatically alter the landscape and politics of New York. Cornelius "Commodore" Vanderbilt had risen from humble beginnings to become a shipping magnate and one of the wealthiest men in the country. After making a fortune in steamships, he bought out the railroad and set about rebuilding Grand Central to reflect his wealth and glory. He let his friend, the tycoon John W. Campbell, set up a private office inside the station starting in 1923. At once, Campbell furnished the place with Oriental rugs, 13th-century Italian furniture, priceless porcelain vases, a huge leadedglass window, and an enormous stone fireplace. Campbell lived in the suburbs, but took great pride in his gorgeous office, and often entertained guests there in the evenings. He used the space until the 1940s.

After Campbell moved out, the room was used as a holding cell for the police, CBS's executive offices, and was left empty and abandoned for a while before it finally reopened to the public as a cocktail bar in 1999. A renovation in 2007 restored the Campbell Apartment to its former glory, making it the epitome of Gilded Age splendor in New York City. You can even see Campbell's original safe, with his name engraved on it, under the fireplace. The cocktail list harkens back to the Jazz Age, with fresh takes on classic drinks, the most celebrated being the Prohibition Punch – a fishbowlsized serving of passion-fruit juices, Appleton Rum Estate VX, and Gran Gala topped with Moët & Chandon champagne. One is all you'll need to feel like a robber baron on par with the Commodore.

KURUMA ZUSHI

Remarkable sashimi flown in from Japan

7 East 47th Street, Midtown East, NY 10017
(212) 317-2802
kurumazushi.com
Monday to Saturday 11:30am–2pm; Sunday 5:30pm–10pm
B, D, F and M trains/7-50 Sts – Rockefeller Center
Expensive

If you're in the market for truly remarkable sushi, look no further than Kuruma Zushi, run by chef Toshihiro Uezu since 1977 on the second floor of an office building in Midtown. A word of warning: sitting at the sushi bar and agreeing to the chef's choice (*omakase*) can run upwards of $300 per person. If that's within your budget, we guarantee that it is worth every penny, with delicacies like *toro* (fatty tuna), *uni* (sea urchin) and king crab made like art in front of you and delivered piece by piece. The sashimi melts in your mouth, full of rich, sea flavors rarely found in ordinary upscale sushi restaurants in New York City. Even the rice is cooked to a level of perfection and temperature. Some of the fish is flown in from Japan daily – Uezu got his start as an apprentice in a restaurant just near the Tsukiji Fish Market in Tokyo.

The experience at Kuruma Zushi is described by critics and food lovers as "euphoric," "transcendent," and "ethereal" and the experience at the sushi bar is made even more memorable with the presence of Uezu himself, who bellows out welcomes in Japanese and English. Throughout the omakase, he'll ask if you want to try other things, like the Russian king crab and it's hard not to resist his enthusiasm and broad smile. He'll also describe the apprenticeship process, notoriously tough in the sushi industry, in front of the latest apprentices. The last one, he says, didn't last too long. Despite the banter, the assistants continue to make sushi with utmost concentration.

The good news for mere mortals is that there's a regular menu too, with lunch at a reasonable $25 for sushi and $30 for sashimi. The tuna lunch specials, three rolls of tuna or a sliced fresh tuna filet over a bed of rice, start at $25. Even with the entry level price point, the quality of the sushi is evident, and the placement of wasabi and garnishes so exact, no extra wasabi is given. There are also classic Japanese appetizers like *sunomono* (fish and seafood marinated in rice vinegar) and *oshinko moriawase* (pickled vegetables).

Decor-wise, the restaurant looks lifted right from Japan. The main attraction is the L-shaped sushi bar, with a smaller sake bar closer to the windows. A large ink-brush painting dominates one wall and an abstract design akin to a Japanese rock garden is behind the sushi bar. You can request seating at tables by the windows or book a private room in advance.

The service is excellent: even the front door opens just at the right moment as you scale the staircase, as there's usually a staff member standing just behind the door. New cups of tea are brought over as you approach the bottom of your current serving and the escalator is called as you sign your bill. And yes, what looks like part of a Japanese temple actually houses the elevator. You'll take the single flight down, sometimes sharing it with people that work upstairs who are unaware of the restaurant, pass by the small security desk and exit back onto the busy Midtown streets.

NORWEGIAN SEAMAN 'S CHURCH COFFEE SHOP

Norwegian snacks in a church sanctuary

317 East 52nd Street, Midtown East, NY 10022
sjomannskirken.no/new-york
Tuesday to Sunday, hours vary
Community gathering place intended for Norwegian expatriates and visitors
E and M trains/Lexington Av or 53rd St
Inexpensive

From the outside, the Norwegian Seaman's Church looks like a government consulate, save for a stained-glass window on the façade. Given the other consulates located on this street in East Midtown, it's easy to walk right past it. But ring the buzzer and you'll first see a cabinet filled with coffee cups that come from many different Norwegian ships. It's a little hint of what comes next, behind the doors of the church sanctuary.

The Norwegian Seaman's Church was formed in 1878 to minister to visiting sailors, serving as a home away from home. Over the years, the church has evolved to serve the Norwegian expatriate community in New York City, functioning more like a cultural organization. As such, tread lightly if visiting: they're welcoming, but it's clear this place is intended for Norwegians. Further proof: the website is completely in Norwegian.

The back of the sanctuary is a café, serving tea, coffee and Norwegian waffles, along with soft drinks. Though there is a wooden counter with a cash register, the café selection is displayed on a long church table covered in a tablecloth. The waffle plus tea or coffee combination is $3, with sugar and jam as topping. You serve yourself on a fun platter with a built-in spot for your coffee cup, featuring the monogram of the church. Once a month, they serve a buffet lunch featuring Norwegian delicacies. Adding to the coziness, there's a brick fireplace (non-functional) and a grandfather clock.

One of the best finds here is the small grocery corner filled with Norwegian staples, including chocolates, licorice, baking ingredients, jams, and packaged soups. There's even a waffle maker.

You'll hear predominantly Norwegian spoken here, making it a real escape. The Norwegian Seaman's Church has been in this location for over twenty years. The upstairs floors are apartments for Norwegians sent to the United States for work. Downstairs, the Trygve Lie gallery has regularly changing exhibitions, and on the mezzanine is a reading room. It's a far cry from when Norwegian churches were on floating boats on the Hudson River but there's still a strong sense of community that can be felt here. A similar, more well-known institution, the Swedish Church on East 48th Street, serves up an affordable lunch of open-faced sandwiches, with cinnamon buns and lingonberry juice.

SAKAGURA

Japanese village beneath a Midtown office

211 East 43rd Street, Midtown East, NY 10017
(212) 953-7253
sakagura.com
Lunch: Monday to Friday 11:30am–2:20pm; dinner: from 6pm every day
4, 5, 6 and 7 trains/Grand Central
Moderate

With its entrance far from the street, Sakagura is one of those truly hidden places.

Open since 1996, it's located in the basement of a nondescript Midtown office building. Pass the security desk through a pristine white lobby and go down the stairs. Cross the threshold of the restaurant and you'll suddenly feel as if you've entered a Japanese village.

The decor is such that diners have the impression they're sitting outside, with interior façades that look like houses, replete with windows, shutters and dormer roofs. Wood and bamboo are the main materials of construction, and though the architecture isn't by any means an exercise of purist Japanese form, the raised level of the sake bar area, a mini Shinto shrine and rice paper dividers give it a homey feel in spite of its basement location.

Cuisine-wise, it's one of the finest for Japanese in New York City at affordable prices. It's also one of those Japanese restaurants where you can order inventive non-sushi dishes and revel in delicious hot foods you might ordinarily only get in Japan. For appetizers, try the Washu beef self-cooked on hot stones, a sea urchin soup with soft boiled egg and salmon roe, the *onsen tamago* (a slow-cooked poached egg in cold soup), the *buta no kakuni* (a special stewed diced-pork dish), or the *chawanmushi* egg custard topped with thickened ponzu soup. For the main course, try the miso stewed beef tongue with shitake mushrooms, spinach, taro potato and daikon radish. There are over 200 types of sake served, including their own exclusive kinds.

The bathrooms at Sakagura are shaped like oversized sake barrels, with interiors decorated like a small apartment. For those that haven't experienced the automatic Japanese toilets, you're in for a treat. The lid will open automatically when you enter, the seats are heated and there are various cleaning and drying options (but you can still do a simple flush).

Upstairs, tucked behind the elevator bank, is a small Japanese bodega, with ready-made take out food from Sakagura. On a visit, don't get confused with the other Japanese restaurant, the Soba Totto Bar, which is right on the street.

Owner Bon Yagi also owns the sake bar Decibel in the East Village, also subterranean, but with a completely different vibe.

BURGER JOINT AT LE PARKER MERIDIEN

Hidden burger joint in an upscale hotel

119 West 56th Street, Midtown East, NY 10019
(212) 708-7414
burgerjointny.com/56thstreet
Sunday to Thursday 11am–11:30pm; Friday and Saturday 11am–midnight
F train/57th St
Moderate

It's been over a decade since Burger Joint first opened up in Le Parker Meridien hotel on 57th Street. By now it's considered one of the mainstays of New York City's burger scene, but the hidden spot still delivers, in part for its famous burgers but also for the juxtaposition between the divey 1970s interior and the posh monumentality of the marble Parker Meridien lobby. There's nothing that reveals Burger Joint's existence, tucked behind thick floor to ceiling velvet curtains, except for a neon burger sign (and the long lines) to denote what lies beyond.

Once inside, you'll be confronted with the scent of burgers, brownies and milkshakes wafting over from the open kitchen. Besides pitchers of Sam Adams beer, the aforementioned are the only items on the menu. Know what you want in advance, or you'll be yelled at and sent to the back of the line. If you freeze, just ask for The Works which puts everything on your burger: lettuce, tomato, onion, sliced pickles, mustard, ketchup, and mayo. The 666 Package gets you a burger, fries and soda for $15.61 (exactly). Two butchers on staff spend most of their time just making burgers for the never-ending crowds, cooking them to that perfect texture. After you order, prepare to battle for a seat.

Because of its popularity, a visit to Burger Joint always shows a crosssection of the New York City population, plus the inevitable tourists. As Le Parker Meridien President Steven Pipes said in an interview with Eater, "What's great about our clientele is that you can't describe it. It crosses all social, economic, geographical possibilities."

Visually, the interior features vinyl booths, 1970s-era wood veneer paneling with sports and movie posters taped haphazardly, and no shortage of graffiti scribbles on the wall. In some ways, anachronism seems to be the theme throughout the hotel: a Gothic-style bar within a neoclassical lobby, a Damien Hirst artwork contrasts with Roman arches. Fun fact: the lobby is actually a public atrium, part of 6½ Avenue, open until midnight every day. Follow 6½ Avenue to cross mid-block within buildings between 51st Street and 57th Street – it's even marked by street signs.

LANTERN'S KEEP

The Iroquois Hotel's little secret

49 West 44th Street, Midtown East, NY 10036
(212) 435-4287
iroquoisny.com/lanternskeep
Monday to Friday 5pm–midnight; Saturday 6pm–1am
B, D, F, M and 7 trains/42nd St – Bryant Park
Moderate

Open in the early 1900s, both the Algonquin and the Iroquois hotels exude the glamor of times past. Inside, the Algonquin has its famed Round Table restaurant, where Dorothy Parker gathered with editors of Vanity Fair and The New Yorker. But the Iroquois has a hidden little jewel box of a cocktail bar called Lantern's Keep. There's no sign for it, but in-the-know imbibers are aware that if the lantern affixed to the Iroquois's façade is lit, they can go inside and have a drink.

Lantern's Keep opened in 2011, but you wouldn't know it from the decor, which looks more like a Parisian Beaux-Arts salon than a New York bar. Chic black paneling contrasts with marble tables and Louis XIV chairs upholstered in powder blue velvet. Impressionist-style paintings of ballerinas adorn the walls. A fireplace adds a touch of elegance. In the corner, a tiny bar (the bartenders call it the cockpit) is equipped with everything needed to whip up craft cocktails.

The youthful head bartender John Ploeser came up through the ranks in his hometown of Madison, Wisconsin before moving to New York to join the opening staff of Perla in the West Village. There he met Theo Lieberman, then head bartender of Milk & Honey, who further trained him in the fine art of making classic cocktails. Along with Meaghan Dorman, Ploeser and his team designed the list of forty original cocktails, from the refreshing Regal Business (gin, grapefruit, honey, lime) to the boozy Double Barrel (rye, dry vermouth, sweet vermouth, angostura and orange bitters). Ploeser has a polite, Midwestern air that makes him instantly likeable and easy to talk to (an important quality in a bartender) and though he studied French literature, he loves the social aspect of bartending and feels at home behind the bar.

Lantern's Keep is like a port of call in a cocktail wasteland. Though the neighborhood has some beautiful historic places, the New Yorkers who work in the surrounding banks and office buildings have few choices besides the ubiquitous Irish pubs and gems like Lantern's Keep, which are still few and far between. Since the bar opened, it has been a haven for post-work cocktails and a happy discovery for tourists staying at the hotel.

WOMEN'S NATIONAL REPUBLICAN CLUB RESTAURANT AND PUB

Founded by New York suffragists

3 West 51st Street, Midtown West, NY 10017
(212) 582-5454
wnrc.org
Monday to Friday, Saturdays seasonally to hotel guests only – check on ext. 2215 for hours/reservations
B, D, F and M trains/47-50 Sts – Rockefeller Center
Moderate

The Women's National Republican Club is a gorgeous clubhouse built on the site of the former home of Andrew Carnegie next to Rockefeller Center. The club was founded by New York suffragists in 1921, but the organization moved into the current building in 1934 after the land was purchased from Carnegie. While it may exude the off-limits vibe of many Gilded Age clubs in New York City, the club is also a hotel with 28 affordable guest rooms (in New York City at least) at about $250 per night.

The pub and restaurant located on level 2M is open to hotel guests. The menu includes bar bites like sliders and chicken wings, appetizers like crab cake and plantain-wrapped sea scallops, along with a large selection of salads, sandwiches, entrees, and desserts.

Though the architecture around the Rockefeller Center area has a tendency towards Art Deco and modernism, the Women's National Republican Club followed the design tastes akin to the private clubs of the era: architect Frederic Rhinelander King designed the building in a Neo-Georgian style both on the exterior and the interior.

According to the National Register of Historic Places, founder and first president Henrietta Wells Livermore "imagined the club as a major force in educating newly enfranchised women voters. From the beginning, the club offered lectures and seminars, and a School of Politics." But in a testament to its open mission, the club didn't have a president for the first 15 years and was run by a collection of women.

Today, several different organizations also share the building, including a physics club and affiliate clubs including the Lambs Club, Squadron A Club, the Netherland Club and the Bond Club. Every Republican President of the United States has visited this building since it opened and the library, called the Calvin Coolidge Library, was donated by the wife of President Coolidge.

The spaces within the club, including grand ballrooms, can also be booked for private events. One room has a wonderful balcony offering a view of St. Patrick's Cathedral on Fifth Avenue and the hidden rooftop gardens at Rockefeller Center.

POSTCRYPT COFFEEHOUSE

One of Columbia University's best-kept secrets

1160 Amsterdam Avenue, Morningside Heights, NY 10027
facebook.com/postcryptcoffeehouseofficial
postcryptcoffeehouse@gmail.com
Friday & Saturday nights during the academic year

n the middle '60s, a reverend decided to clean up a 200-year-old church basement storage room, buy a few tables, build a stage, name after philosopher Soren Kierkegaard's "Concluding Unscientific ostscript" and start what has become one of Columbia University's est-kept secrets.

For nearly six decades now, Postcrypt Coffeehouse has continued to perate out of its little 30-person hollow beneath the university campus' . Paul's Chapel on Amsterdam Avenue. Over the years, a host of lobally renowned acts, including Jeff Buckley and Suzanne Vega, have raced the homemade stage installed by Rev. John Cannon – who was, the time, a campus chaplain – and his helper, one Dotty Sutherland. ince its birth in 1964, the stonewalled subterranean saloon has been acked with countless students and innumerable numbers of people ave walked by overhead, never knowing there was a live show being erformed beneath their feet.

When returning to the underground den of acoustic appreciation here are no microphones at Postcrypt), alumni often comment on how nchanged it all seems. While time marches on elsewhere, the stage as stayed exactly the same – indeed, it is to this day the original one. mosaic bar constructed by Sutherland is still used to serve tea and offee, which patrons drink at the original chairs and tables. An over-oor box of unknown origin with the handwritten word "Postcrypt" has lso stood the test of time, as have the many regulars who return time nd again to the space.

Every Friday and Saturday night during the academic year, students nd strangers alike are invited to venture down free of charge and xperience some music, some warm (albeit nonalcoholic) beverages, nacks and company in the timeless chamber. Entry is granted on a first-ome, first-served basis and it remains free and entirely student-run.

"The Postcrypt offers no refuge from intimacy. It is at once ntimidating and exhilarating for a performer to know they will have o choice but to look into the eyes of the audience that has come to e them give something of themselves," reads a 1991 clipping from ast Folk Musical Magazine which was included in a zine to celebrate ne venue's 50th anniversary. Another snippet from the zine recalls the npressive amount of open flames and melted candle-filled wine bottles Postcrypt in 2000, as well as the popularity of a bar snack served at ne time called GORP, or "Good Old Raisins and Peanuts."

Since Postcrypt's inception, another student-run Columbia venue – nis one an exhibition space – has also adopted the name: Postcrypt Art allery currently operates out of the university's Dodge Hall.

THE GARRYOWEN AT THE 69TH REGIMENT ARMORY

Hidden bar for the military

68 Lexington Avenue, Murray Hill, NY 10024
Open only to military personnel and their guests
Armory sometimes open for events
6 train/28th St
Inexpensive

The 69th Infantry Regiment, known in popular culture as "The Fighting Irish," was initially an all-Irish brigade founded to train Irish immigrants in America to free Ireland from British control. The regiment has had an illustrious history fighting in the Civil War, World War I, World War II and the Iraq war. Wild Bill Donovan, the WWI Medal of Honor awardee, was also part of the 69th and went on to be in charge of the OSS, a forerunner to the CIA. The 69th was also one of the first responders at Ground Zero, going in against orders. Their motto, "Gentle when stroked, fierce when provoked," references the Irish wolfhounds on their coat of arms. There's even a James Cagney movie, "The Fighting Irish," about them.

The regiment's landmarked armory on Lexington Avenue and 25th Street is still active and you can get in when they open for events. In fact, the 1904 building is landmarked because the building hosted the first New York City Armory Show in 1913, not for its military history.

The architects of the armory were Hunt & Hunt, who also designed one of the Vanderbilt mansions on Fifth Avenue. The immense arched drill hall has remnants of wonderful wood auditorium seats on the second floor. There are also historical artifacts from the regiment's involvement in various global conflicts in glass cases throughout the entrance hall and in the main reception room. The wooden doors inside and at the entrance are reinforced and resistant to pistol fire, a remnant of the security needs when the armory was built.

But the real hidden gem inside this armory is The Garryowen, a bar that began as an officers' club but now welcomes military personnel and their guests. The wood-paneled space, named after the regiment's marching tunes, got its current look around 1962, but existed in an earlier form prior to that. A marble fireplace is flanked with massive artillery while personalized beer steins line the walls, flipped upside down for enlistees who are gone. There's also a relic of the World Trade Center framed on the wall. One of the biggest days at The Garryowen is St. Patrick's Day where upwards of 400 to 500 people come by. Despite the rowdiness, we're told only one person has ever been banned from the bar (for life). The offering is simple with beers on tap and standard cocktails. The real experience when visiting The Garryowen is about the stories you'll hear.

RAINES LAW ROOM AT THE WILLIAM

Drinks in a stately brownstone

24 East 39th Street, Murray Hill, NY 10016
raineslawroom.com
Monday to Wednesday 5pm–1am; Thursday to Saturday 5pm–2am
4, 5, 6, 7 and S trains/Grand Central
Moderate

The second location of Raines Law Room at The William, a luxury extended-stay hotel for the modern traveler, may be even more efitting its name than the original spot. After all, the famous loophole in ne Raines Law of 1896, which prevented the sale of alcohol on Sundays xcept in hotels, prompted a flurry of saloons to add furnished rooms.

As such, co-owner Yves Jadot chose the location of Raines Law Room eliberately, after a long search. The William is located in the former ome of the Williams Club, a private club for the alumni of Williams ollege in Massachusetts. The two stately interconnected brownstones ere an appropriately historical setting for the East Coast liberal arts ollege, founded in 1793, the same year George Washington was sworn as the first President of the United States. In 2010, the Williams Club ecamped to the Princeton Club's building on West 43rd Street and the wnhouses were renovated by Jadot.

Raines Law Room is technically located on the parlor floor but it's ccessed through the basement bar, The Shakespeare Pub. From there, e host takes you through a door marked "No Admittance," through elvet curtains and up a staircase. Because of the townhouse layout, aines Law Room is split into two rooms across from each other. ne room contains the bar and a few alcoves of seating, separated by ng curtains. For those familiar with the original Raines Law Room, e bar room is probably most reminiscent of their first location. The arlor room across the way is designed like a house library, with backlit ookshelves, wing chairs and tufted couches. Candles illuminate the ark marble fireplace, while suggestive paintings harken back to the rothels of an earlier New York. Also look closely at the wallpaper and hat look like floral flourishes are actually bodies of naked women, a esign element introduced at the original Raines Law Room. Also like e original location, service bells built into the walls notify the wait aff you're ready to order.

The cocktail menu is similar to the original spot too but with more ldfashioned influence, with head bartender Meaghan Dorman in harge of cocktail development at both. Instead of a menu organized by pirit type, there are three simple categories: Bright & Fresh, Stirred & trong, and With a Hint of Spice. Then there's the Choose Your Own dventure: Old Fashioned where you pick your bitters, sweeteners, and pirits. You can also order a specially curated menu of small bites from he Peacock restaurant, also inside The William, while at your seats.

This outpost of Raines Law Room at The William is a nice addition o the Murray Hill and Midtown East neighborhoods and a perfect omplement to the hotel, but the original location has more of the old-chool speakeasy feel. As the menu says: choose your own adventure.

HONORABLE WILLIAM WALL CLUBHOUSE

Floating club in New York Harbor

myc.org
May to October; Dates and hours vary
Departs from Pier 25 in Manhattan and Liberty Harbor Marina, Jersey City next to Surf City Restaurant
Affordable

The Honorable William Wall (aka the "Willy Wall") is the floating clubhouse of the Manhattan Yacht Club, anchored in the New York harbor just near Ellis Island. The open air bar has incredible views of downtown Manhattan and the Statue of Liberty (and neighboring Brooklyn and New Jersey, of course). Indeed, the clubhouse was designed specifically for taking in the sailboat races and you'll notice it is more of a viewing platform and barge rather than a sleek yacht. To get to the William Wall, you take the Admiral's Launch, a United States Coast Guard certified vintage motorboat from either Pier 25 in Manhattan or Liberty Harbor Marina in Jersey City (before 2015, it left from North Cove Marina in Battery Park). The red-hulled boat fits 40 comfortably.

The secret here is that you don't have to be a member of the club to experience the clubhouse: it's simply an $18 roundtrip launch fee, payable online. You can also just wait standby starting at 7:30pm if tickets are sold out. Manhattan Sailing Club members get to go to the front of the line, but that's usually not an issue for the 149-person capacity clubhouse except during peak periods.

The drinks are affordable and the offering is straightforward because the experience is ostensibly the races. Wine, beer, liquor and standard mixed drinks are available – served in plastic cups – but no cocktails. The chill factor is accentuated by the fact that you can bring your own picnics, or order food from Surf City in Jersey City, which gets brought to the clubhouse by the launch boat. The races begin at a buoy near the William Wall, go up the Hudson River and back, turn around in the cove behind the clubhouse, and return to the same starting point.

The first level of the William Wall is the formal clubhouse, a wood-beamed space outfitted with club chairs and a built in bar. Though this space was once exclusive to club members, it is now open to the general public as well. Here you will find memorabilia of the club's history and a small library. Framed is a letter from the Yacht Club of Monaco designating the Manhattan Sailing Club as the first ambassador of the Spirit of Tuiga Club, presided over by HSH Prince Albert II of Monaco. But the open-air top level, with the central bar, is where the action is.

And who is William Wall, you may ask? By all accounts he was rather "honorable," serving as a U.S. Congressman during the Civil War, consulted on by Abraham Lincoln in regards to the use of the Brooklyn Navy Yard. Born in Philadelphia, Wall was trained as a ropemaker and set up his own business in Williamsburg in the 1820s, where he became a key figure in local government.

Getting out on the water, especially during the summer in New York City, is always a special treat, and the Honorable William Wall is one of the most affordable and unique ways to do that.

PATENT PENDING

A speakeasy in the back of a coffee shop

49 W 27th Street, Nomad, NY 10001
(212) 689-4002
patentpendingnyc.com
Daily 5pm–2am

Don't be fooled by the darkness: the closed appearance of the coffee shop entry is part of the shtick. The café front to this bar may serve Java during the day, but by night it's a transitional space, used to host the line that often forms as patrons wait to access the main attraction.

Past the coffee counter and through a hinged wall of menus, two neat lines of blue barstools and dark green booths await in front of a black, mirrored bar. This is Patent Pending, the electricity-themed bar beyond Patent Coffee.

And beyond Patent Pending is yet another venue, a speakeasy within a speakeasy. Known as The Lab, it is accessed by going to the back of Patent Pending and locating the hidden cavern connected via a natural arch. This even smaller chamber seats 30, has two bartending stations and a separate bathroom. It is also available for private rental.

Both bars share a menu of cocktails which push both the envelope of complexity and price point. A mezcal and rum-based Impossible Idea will run you $33, while the Eclectic Messiah, made with small-batch bourbon, costs $32. Those looking to shell out slightly less can pick from numerous $20 options, many with thematically appropriate names like Cosmic Rays (American gin, dry vermouth, green apple) or Radio Waves (tequila, mezcal, rum, Thai chile).

An arguably greater work of art than the drinks, though, is the menu itself. More zine than list, these booze brochures truly elevate the menu game to an uncommon level, and in an increasingly paperless era ruled by the QR code.

"Welcome to the cellar of the Radio Wave Building," the vintage-looking pamphlet begins. "This is the building in which Nikola Tesla lived and performed his experiments on radio waves, transmitting them to his laboratory near present-day Trinity Church in downtown Manhattan. The 'waves' which guided you here (GPS) and surround you now (WiFi) were envisioned by Tesla more than a century ago."

Further building history follows alongside an illustrated drinks list. The pamphlet concludes with an appendix and a multi-page list of U.S. patents granted to Tesla. It's available for purchase for $33 a pop.

History is not only on the menu at Patent Pending – it's also in the walls: while building out the bar, staff came upon old artifacts from the original construction back in the late 19th century. Found objects included oyster shells, milk and liquor bottles, playing cards, matchbooks, newspaper snippets and articles of clothing. A whole former world, unearthed.

GEORGE BANG BANG

To enter, guests must walk past diners at a Korean comfort food restaurant

13 East 30th St, Nomad, NY 10016
(646) 707-0420
gbbnyc.com
Monday to Sunday, 6pm–2am

In a meta twist, this speakeasy is speakeasy-themed. Opened in 2022, George Bang Bang offers creative cocktail creations in a sultry Koreatown space.

The name is a take on a Korean slang phrase meaning, more or less, "Whatever." It can be applicable to both close friends and enemies, the menu explains, adding it "reflects a free-spirited, unapologetic attitude and a refusal to conform."

George Bang Bang is, however, rebellious mostly in name alone: The space and its menu are meticulously curated.

To enter, guests must walk past diners at Okdongsik (translation: "single-item restaurant"), the Michelin-approved, Seoul-born Korean comfort food restaurant chain and soup specialist. The door to George Bang Bang is visible from the street, through the glass front, at the end of the bar — yet it's sufficiently well-camouflaged, blending in with the striped wall around it, that it can be easily missed.

The brightly lit soupery contrasts intensely with the darkness beyond.

Inside the long, narrow space, the moody design is in fact significantly inspired by the 1997 film "Titanic," according to the bar's owner. Behind the bar, the backlit red liquor shelves are meant to pay homage to the glamour of the ship.

In the corner, by the dimly lit bathroom (which features a checkered floor and a haunted energy) is an armless statue. A stalagmite of wax sits beneath an ever-dripping candle (quite the choice, considering all the wood).

Film negatives hang at the front, hinting subtly at the movie-heavy theme, which continues on to the cocktail menu.

There's the truffle honey-forward 500 Days of Summer, the gin-based Grand Budapest Hotel and the Little Miss Sunshine, which includes bee pollen, egg white, and ginger.

Perhaps most unique is The Most Beautiful Moment In Life, which also happens to be the name of a series of albums by the South Korean boy band BTS, and features lavender-infused rum, coconut water and cream cheese. It is, perhaps surprisingly, very tasty, albeit a very unique mix of densities.

The food menu is sparse but there are some light bites on offer, including wasabi pork shumai and homemade beef jerky.

LITTLE DIPPER

The entrance to this astrologically-minded bar is easily missed

135 West 30th Street, Nomad, NY 10001
littledippernyc.com
Thursday, Friday and Saturday 5pm "till late"

Little Dipper bar caters directly to the astrologically-minded, offering a star sign-themed experience in an ironically underground space.

The entrance is easily missed – a painted fire door, propped open next to a single velvet-roped stanchion. Through it is a set of stairs, the walls painted in neon acrylic and glowing beneath a blacklight.

Downstairs, in the basement of the Courtyard by Marriott Chelsea, is a hotel-friendly bar designed to be sleek and approachable, but with the delightful horoscope-focused twist.

Mirrored glass greets you upon entry, and a large screen is affixed to the ceiling, twinkling with stars. Zodiac constellation sconces adorn the walls and there's a variety of plush velvet seating options, all in a galactic palette of black, blue, purple and gold.

The cocktails are divided by element and named for each astrological symbol, with an accompanying name (for Capricorn, The Bitter Resolve; for Pisces, the Lunar Lullabye), one line quote ("Grace in balance, Libra lives where beauty meets truth") and of course, the ingredients, the latter of which has no obvious connection to the star sign (who is to say that all Geminis should find a vodka and green tea soju-based drink appealing?). They tend on the sweeter side, and there's also limited wine, beer and sake options.

In the corner is a mobile hand roll cart. Given 24 hours' notice, Little Dipper also offers a full 12-course, hand-selected omakase meal, with a vegetarian omakase option to boot.

No notice is necessary for the single rolls, though, nor the rest of the limited menu (BBQ oysters, uni tots and roasted eggplant toast, to name a few).

Upstairs, on the ground floor of the hotel, is Little Dipper's three-year-old sister bar, Goldie's Tavern, a surprisingly sleek sports bar accessible from its subterranean star-sign sibling via an interior stairwell.

The inspiration for the Little Dipper, which opened in May 2024, came not from the stars above but the space below: "Being at the bottom of a hotel, you end up with a lot of space," explained Wayne Gravesande, general manager of both Little Dipper and Goldie's. "We just had so much space, it was like, let's find a cool concept to throw here and see what we can do in Midtown."

One of the bar's owners knew somebody who could do the ceiling video screen, "and everything kind of just organically came together" from there.

GANESH TEMPLE CANTEEN

Dosas for the gods

45-47 Bowne Street, Flushing, Queens, NY 11355
(718) 460-8484
nyganeshtemplecanteen.com
Daily 8:30am–9pm
7 and 7X trains/Flushing – Main St
Inexpensive

Across from a row of single-family houses in Flushing is a large building with an entrance so intricately carved, it looks straight from a temple in India. The Ganesh Temple, as it's colloquially known, was founded in 1970 with the current building dating from 1977. Its official name is the Hindu Temple Society of North America, named such because when founded in 1970 it was the first and only traditional Hindu temple in the country.

But the story goes back much further to America's colonial period. Predating the Bill of Rights, a document known as the Flushing Remonstrance was signed by Flushing settlers in protest of Dutch persecution of Quakers, extending "the law of love, peace and liberty," beyond Christians to all faiths and backgrounds. Flushing farmer John Bowne soon welcomed Quakers to meet at his house, which still stands.

More than 350 years later, this same street, named after Bowne, now includes a synagogue, a Sikh gurdwara, a Chinese church, the Ganesh temple, and another Hindu temple.

The Ganesh temple is "permanently consecrated," meaning there's a permanent staff of priests that manage the holy statues. The stone deities on the exterior of the building were reconsecrated in 2009 with an impressive nearly week-long ritual. A cow and a 37-year-old elephant were part of the festivities – an homage to Ganesha, the elephant-headed god.

But downstairs is a canteen serving up dosas, masalas, and mango lassi so good it warranted a visit from Anthony Bourdain. There are 17 variations of dosas, and an additional four varieties available only on weekends. A nearby Hindu resident says that the canteen was started to compete with the Dosa Hutt next door, but the official story from the temple president is that the canteen got its start when a chef was hired in 1993 to cook *naivedyams* (food offerings) for the gods, but was soon cooking for the worshippers too.

The all-vegetarian canteen is open seven days a week from morning until night with Ganesha in gold overseeing the basement dining space. Afterwards grab some desserts at the sweets shop in the Swaminarayan Hindu temple just down the street or explore the Golden Mall, a subterranean Chinese food court also in Flushing.

FINBACK BREWERY TASTING ROOM

Inventive beers in Queens

7801 77th Avenue, Glendale, Queens, NY 11385
info@finbackbrewery.com
finbackbrewery.com
Thursday and Friday 4pm–9pm; Saturday 1pm–8pm; Sunday 1pm–7pm
L and M trains/Myrtle – Wykoff, then Q55 bus
Moderate

This gem of a tasting room is worth the trek to Glendale, Queens and getting there is part of the adventure. From Manhattan you take the L or the M train to the Myrtle–Wyckoff station at the literal border of Brooklyn and Queens, transfer to the Q55 bus and then walk through a residential neighborhood in Glendale. Suddenly on 77th Avenue, you'll encounter some warehouses. In the winter, the garage doors will all be closed and the only hint that something is going on may be the "Yes, we're open!" sign taped to one of the unmarked doors.

For the (epi)curious, opening this particular door on the otherwise uniform industrial block will lead to a beautifully designed tasting room and bar retrofitted into the loading dock of Finback Brewery. The bar is lined with bright silver metal stools and the wooden tables and benches in the main seating area were handmade by the Finback team. The wooden tap handles, each stamped with the Finback logo, are built into a marble wall. Above, a mirror doubles as a menu where they write and cross out brews as they're available. From the bar, you can see right into the brewery itself, with its mash tanks and grain silos. Sometimes the staff zips through the tasting room on skateboards, carrying empty plastic barrels.

Owners Basil Lee and Kevin Stafford began as home brewers, and it's evident in the inventive mix of flavors that are in Finback beers. If you're looking for rich, unique flavors, this is the brewery for you–with sour beers and others flavored with the likes of jalapeño, coconut, mango, and plum. The Double Sess(ion) is brewed with Szechuan peppercorn, chamomile, and ginger: a great choice as a summer beer or for those that like beers less hoppy. The Fort Tildenist beer is brewed with green tea and lemon zest. Finback beers have clever names like Coasted Toconut, Cat Love, and Plumb & Proper, along with seasonal beers and Finback IPA that's always on tap.

In the back rooms of the warehouse, Finback is aging beer in bourbon, whiskey, and wine barrels. In late 2014, Finback released a barrel-aged BQE beer brewed with cocoa nibs from Mast Brothers Chocolate and coffee from Native Coffee Roasters in Queens, along with another barrel-aged beer called Smoke Detection.

Beers are currently only available on tap at bars in the greater New York City area and visiting the Finback Brewery tasting room is a great opportunity to hear directly from the team that heads up this small local business. Plus, there's always free popcorn from the vintage machine in the corner.

DUTCH KILLS

An unmarked gem in an industrial zone

27-24 Jackson Avenue, Long Island City, Queens, NY 10017
(718) 383-2724
dutchkillsbar.com
Seven days a week 5pm–2am
E, M and R trains/Queens Plaza; E, M, 7 and G trains/Court St
Moderate

In a nondescript two-floor brick building between a transmission shop and a taxi lot, Dutch Kills is an unmarked gem, save for a neon BAR sign and a plywood sign denoting "Blissville Kitchen." The area in Long Island City, formerly a forgotten industrial stretch off the Queensboro Bridge, is undergoing a transformation. Interspersed amidst the auto repair shops and taxi services are new highrise glass rentals and condos. But this bar, opened in 2009, predated much of the gentrification taking place, distinguishing itself from other speakeasies through its comprehensive liquor selection and use of fresh ingredients in a cocktail menu that appeals to those who enjoy spirits.

Despite nearby development, walking into Dutch Kills still feels like entering a long-lost world. You'll first encounter the main seating area with private wooden booths that seat anywhere from two to six, divided from each other by red curtains. The experience at Dutch Kills is about intimacy and the architecture reflects that. The same wood paneling on the wall continues onto the low ceiling, giving the space a real, old-school tavern feel. You'd never guess that the same space used to be a fishmonger's office and cold-storage facility.

In the lofty back room is a long wooden bar with a silver cash register. The bar stools are circular and spin, like in a New York luncheonette but upgraded. A small skylight lets in a little daylight in the otherwise dim space. The numerous bottles behind the bar are organized by type, with all the classics plus absinthe, amaros, and mezcal.

The vibe at Dutch Kills has always been deliberately divey and fun. The bar room is decorated with vintage memorabilia including a jukebox, money from Europe, religious art and old advertisements. Mixed in are modern-day additions, like the menu served at the birthday of one of Dutch Kills' long-time patrons. Mismatched light fixtures hang from the ceiling, but work with the eclectic decor.

The drink menu offers cocktails directly descended from New York City classics from the 1880s to the 1940s. There's an offering of hot drinks too, including Hot Toddy, Irish Coffee, and Mulled Cider. Dutch Kills bartenders can also make drinks based on your preferences or, for the curious, let them do their magic. On a visit pay attention to the glasses: the round cocktail coupes are often used in bars in Sasha Petraske's group and predate triangular Martini glasses. Water is served in Art Deco silver julep cups with metal straws.

And the name Dutch Kills? The kills, meaning a channel or creek in Dutch, refer to the former waterways of the area that have long been paved over. As of 2024, Dutch Kills' upper floor is home to a live music venue with its own bar called Debbie's, named for the ghost employees believe has been long haunting Dutch Kills.

THE LITTLE SHOP

One of New York City's more surprising hidden watering holes

252 Front Street, Seaport, NY, 10038
(646) 360-4650
thelittleshopny.com
Open 5pm daily

At Manhattan's watery edge, in the shadow of the Brooklyn Bridge, on a cobblestoned portion of Front Street sits The Little Shop. Walk through its blue double doors and the space feels true to the name: A particularly well-curated, upscale market offering a notably high-and low-brow mix of buyables ranging from potato chips to small-batch chocolates and high-end deodorant. The floor looks unfinished; the ceiling has exposed beams; the contrasts are strong yet subtle: What a weird bodega.

Walk between the back aisles, though, and a portion of the white wall slides aside to reveal an intimate, sumptuously wall-papered, living room-like space serving up involved cocktails and light snacks.

The two-part business, which bills itself as a purveyor "of fine and junk foods," has been slinging coffee and cocktails since December 2019 and going strong. Since opening, it has made and maintained a name for itself as a quality drink spot that is both chic and semi-secret in a part of New York that is known for being other things, but not that.

"We've had day-time shop regulars who have shopped with us for months who have no idea there's a bar in the back, and we also have bar customers who don't believe the shop is real (even though we stock over 1,000 items)," says The Little Shop co-owner Anna Bazhenova, who started the business with longtime Seaport resident Philippe Boujnah. The partners met at an ad agency.

One of the funnier regular occurrences at The Little Shop, Bazhenova says, is when someone brings a date there, "and you see the date being confused as to why they're in a corner store, but then get excited when the cocktail bar is revealed."

Indeed, this South Street Seaport speakeasy is one of New York City's more surprising hidden watering holes, both because the bar entrance is better camouflaged than most, and because the back room's vibe is earnestly intimate and tastefully put together in a way few spaces are in this particularly Disneyfied, touristy nabe.

Perhaps because of this contrast to its surroundings, Bazhenova says it gets a "true variety of guests, from tourists to local office workers to neighborhood regulars to the occasional celebrity."

© Alix Piorun

APRÈS-SKI FONDUE CHALET AT CAFÉ SELECT

Swiss ski chalet through a kitchen

212 Lafayette Street, Soho, NY 10012
(212) 925-9322
cafeselectnyc.com
info@cafeselectnyc.com
Daily from 8am; weekends 9am
6 train/Spring St
Moderate

There isn't a moment in Café Select that isn't impeccably thought through, from the Rolex train station clock (one of three in the world) to the spray paint letters in the bathroom that tell employees to wash their hands. This holistic, almost narrative, design concept extends to what would normally be considered an unusable space – a boiler room behind the kitchen. Owner Serge Becker, the man behind New York institutions like The Box and La Esquina, chose to make it a hidden restaurant from the very beginning when Café Select opened in 2008.

The Après-Ski Fondue Chalet is exactly what it sounds like – a hidden ski chalet accessed through the kitchen of Café Select, if you dare to walk through the door that says "No Entry, Employees Only." Open the door at the back of the kitchen and be suddenly transported to the Swiss Alps. Fondue (in numerous variations) is on the menu, along with everything else that's available in the café out front. You can even get hot mulled wine here, made in a small pot atop a portable burner, just like the lunchtime refreshment popular on European ski outings. This version is mulled with orange, pomegranate, and five different spices: nutmeg, cloves, black pepper, cinnamon, and star anise.

If the front room at Café Select wears its curation on its sleeve, the back room is decidedly loose and unpretentious. There are skis, boots and poles, sleds, and snowboards hanging around the room and nestled in corners. There's an old-school feel, with narrow skis (none of those parabolic ones), colored Christmas lights, and vintage ski posters. A small staircase leads up to a wooden balcony with decorative balustrades, like those found on a Swiss chalet. The corner bar, replete with a few stools, is just a metal slab and the liquor shelves are made of simple wooden boards.

The small space lends itself to coziness, but not towards loudness like so many New York City establishments. The aim is simple here: good bistro food and a cool vibe. This means that Café Select swings towards particular types of clientele – models and fashionistas on one end of the spectrum, and hip everyday regulars on the other – but predominantly New Yorkers. True to the restaurant's mission, the staff is friendly and unpretentious, moving between the two worlds with ease and spirit.

And the best part – in summer, the chalet turns into an oyster shack. "It's Montauk instead of Montblanc," says manager Benoit Cornet. The ski paraphernalia is replaced by fish nets, bikinis, buoys, and lifesavers. It even has a different name for the summer months: Cervantes' Oyster Shack and Bar.

LA ESQUINA

Chic Mexican brasserie under a taco shop

114 Kenmare Street, Soho, NY 10012
(646) 613-7100
esquinanyc.com
Daily 6pm–2am
6 train/Spring St
Moderate

The name of this place ("the corner" in Spanish) would have you think it's just your average little corner taqueria. From the outside, it looks very casual, like an old Mexican diner with corrugated tin siding and a neon sign. It's not a front, per se. You could certainly come here and just get some tacos to go. But then you might get curious about where the people disappearing through the door inside the narrow taqueria are going.

If you have a reservation or are lucky enough to get in without one, the host will open the door for you and you'll walk downstairs, through the kitchen (where the Latino chefs are assembling taquitos and ceviche), and into the main brasserie. Behind the long bar, bottles of tequila and mezcal stand at attention. Upstairs, everything is bright, but here it's dimly lit, though not too dark to see the very sensual painting of an odalisque lounging above the sofas. Past a row of iron bars, the dining room feels a bit like a dungeon, but with better food. The tables and chairs are made from a dark wood, and blue-and-white tiles form playful mosaics on the walls. Candles poised around the room are dripping in wax. A thumping soundtrack of pop music sets a party mood.

La Esquina is known for its margaritas and they deliver. Espolón reposado tequila, triple sec, fresh lime juice, and passion fruit or blood-orange juice comes blended together in a goblet with a salted rim and slices of lime and orange. There are other cocktails, including one with vodka, one with gin, and one with bourbon, but most feature tequila or mezcal as the base, and rightfully so. They're the perfect complement to the Mexican street food on the menu. There's the classic *elotes callejeros* (grilled corn on the cob smothered in mayonnaise, *cotija* cheese, and lime juice), ceviche and *queso fundido* (melted chihuahua cheese with pumpkin seeds and chile de arbol) that arrives in a small cast-iron pan with plantain chips for dipping. And of course, there are tacos in all varieties: grilled steak, chicken, fish of the day, cheese, veal tongue, carnitas, and slow-roasted pulled pork. Each order comes with two tacos, which arrive on a wooden platter. The more you order, the larger the platter that comes out. At around $5 per taco, the price is the only clue that you're definitely not in Mexico City here.

MI PEQUEÑO CHINANTLA

A hit among foodies and fans of the hidden

4011 5th Avenue, Sunset Park, 11232
(718) 972-1578
Monday to Saturday 11 am–1pm; Sunday 10 am–9:30pm

Smell stew? See a deer's head? You're in the right place. Tucked away in the back of a Sunset Park bodega, this miniscule Mexican eatery was built in homage to the owner's native town and, over the years, has become a hit among foodies and fans of the hidden.

The appeal is obvious for both parties: the itty-bitty eatery is unmarked, uniquely full of taxidermy and serves up generous portions of its sprawling, homestyle food.

While the La Union Deli Grocery awning announces that it sells Salvadoran products, it makes no mention of the beloved operation happening in the back. A handmade Spanish menu listing taped to the front window above the shelves of fresh fruit, though, does hint that more than advertised awaits within.

Once inside La Union Deli, the narrow space is packed with regional snacks and staples, a deli counter and, above a door in the back, the deer's head (it's hard to miss). Through here lies the second food establishment located within this ground-floor business: Mi Pequeño Chinantla.

Inside, the walls are covered with tchotchkes, mirrors, traditional art and a number of mounted taxidermy pieces. There's another deer, a wolf, a lone set of horns, and a rather menacing-looking bobcat, all watching over the little operation. A few plants perch on a shelf, peering into the bodega and the sunshine beyond its door.

A sprawling, handwritten menu hangs from the ceiling and lists an enormous number of order possibilities. There are *picaditas* (corn cakes served with salsa and queso), a traditional soup called *mole de panza*, a crowd-favorite weekend *barbacoa* special, quesadillas and taco options galore but the heart of this operation are the tamales and the *guisado*. The latter, a beyond hearty stew, changes daily, as does the availability of the rest of the written menu, not to mention the unwritten one. There's an additional menu on Saturdays and Sundays. (Really, it's best to just ask what's on deck that day and go with that.)

There are extremely limited seating options inside but, if it's a nice day, Sunset Park – for which the neighborhood is named – is less than a block away, and the expansive Green-Wood Cemetery is a short walk north.

Mi Pequeño Chinantla faces steep local competition in a neighborhood dense with affordable Mexican bites, but you'd be hard pressed to find a rival as eclectically decorated.

OVERSTORY

Breathtaking views from the former third-tallest building in the world

64th floor of 70 Pine Street, Financial District, 10005
(212) 339-3963
overstory-nyc.com
Tuesday to Saturday 5:45pm–midnight

Everything tastes better from above, and little pairs better with sky-high cocktail prices than a view to match. When the Financial District's landmarked 70 Pine Street was completed in 1932 it was, at 952 feet and 67 stories, the third-tallest building in the world, and its highest floors were reserved for use by executives. Today, the 64th floor of the skyscraper is home to Overstory, where reservations are available but walk-ins are welcome.

The less than 600-square-foot interior features an underlit brass-and-marble bar surrounded by plush stools which appear rather cloud-like at dusk. But the most elegant furnishings in the world couldn't possibly compare to the view from the wraparound terrace. Out here on the Art Deco railing-enclosed deck, hundreds of feet above Manhattan, New York is spread to the horizon from 360 degrees. The views are so breathtaking that the bar is arguably more of an observation deck with drinks service.

To access Overstory, guests take an elevator up from its red marble lobby to its much more expensive and exclusive sister restaurant, Saga, before being escorted up a travertine stairwell to the bar's indoor area one flight up.

While a meal just a story below costs a base level of $295, cocktails at Overstory are comparatively not bad at $24 a pop. The most affordable drink option, a 12oz. can of cider, costs $11. Limited food offerings include oysters, royal sturgeon caviar and BBQ lamb buns.

Meanwhile, at Saga, the opulence is endless as, seemingly, is the amount of money that can be spent in a single sitting. The restaurant occupies four full stories of the building and boasts three terraces and a 56-seat dining room. This square footage was originally designed to be a private apartment for the founder of Cities Service Company, today known as Citgo (the oil and gasoline giant).

"Saga" is an acronym for venue creators James Kent and Jeff Katz's children's names. The layout is intended to give the impression of being not at a restaurant but a very rich friend's house: diners are invited to explore the sprawling indoor and outdoor space, and certain courses in the seasonal tasting menu are served plated while others are intended for communal consumption. The exorbitant price tag is attached not just to a meal but to an experience.

The residential building is additionally host to a ground-floor restaurant by Kent and Katz (who are also behind Overstory). Being at the building's base, Crown Shy can't boast the views of its sister venues above, but it does have 16-foot-ceiling windows, an open kitchen and a Michelin star.

© Alix Piorun

BAR CENTRALE

Nightcap spot for Broadway stars

324 West 46th Street, Theater District, NY 10036
(212) 581-3030
barcentrale.nyc
Daily 5pm "til late"
N, Q and R trains/49th St; C and E trains/50th St
Moderate

Up a flight of steps and behind a nondescript townhouse door, Bar Centrale feels a world away from the hustle and bustle of the Theater District. Outside, chaos reigns, inside, the bar is a safe haven. Broadway actors come here for a nightcap after their shows, knowing they can count on the staff's discretion.

Bar Centrale is definitely not a period piece like Sardi's, Barbetta, and other longstanding spots in the neighborhood, but there are nods to the area's history throughout the space. When you first walk in and pass through a velvet curtain, you're face to face with a coat check manned by an attendant (quite rare these days). Black and white photos grace the walls, and a small TV above the bar plays old movies, like "Sabrina". There are booths and black tables, one of which has ticket stubs and matchbooks under glass. Even the bathroom has blown-up black and white vintage photos of Times Square and nearby Hell's Kitchen. It's glamorous, but not showy; a bit retro, but not put-on. The whole place has an air of mystery – you never know who you might see.

The menu is equally distinguished but unfussy. There's wine, beer, and classic cocktails for people who don't need to look at a menu, but just order their Tanqueray Martini with a twist because that's how they always take their Martinis. Ask for one and the bartender will serve it in a small glass, with a mini carafe that keeps the rest of your drink on ice, so you never have to go through the agony of imbibing a warm cocktail. Bar fare includes classics like oysters, shrimp cocktails, and caviar, plus lobster quesadillas, vegetarian samosas, and Chinese dumplings. Service is courteous and attentive.

Speakeasies and hidden bars are relatively rare in Midtown. Perhaps because historically, development started downtown and slowly worked its way up. During Prohibition – when bars were forcibly driven underground – this area was relatively uncharted territory. Aside from Barbetta – the oldest restaurant in New York City continually run by the same family – this area was just developing in the early 20th century. It wasn't until 1973 that 46th Street came to be known as Restaurant Row, thanks to Mayor John Lindsay. The fact that Bar Centrale is hidden behind a townhouse façade lets actors come and go in peace, even while fans and paparazzi shuffle in and out of the other restaurants on the block.

BAR AND DINING ROOM AT THE SOCIETY OF ILLUSTRATORS

Upper East Side arts club

128 East 63rd Street, Upper East Side, NY 10065
societyillustrators.org
Museum: Tuesday 10am–8pm, Wednesday to Friday 10am–5pm, Saturday 12pm–4 pm
Sketch nights: Tuesday and Thursday 6:30pm–9:30pm
Monthly brunches and dinners open to the public
F train/Lexington Av or 63rd St; 4, 5, 6, N, Q and R trains/Lexington Av or 59th St

The Society of Illustrators is one of those hidden gems that even some of its neighbors don't realize exists – particularly the bar and dining room on the third floor of this Upper East Side club. Yet, the organization has been active since 1901 and in its current home, an 1875 carriage house, since 1935.

Though the Society of Illustrators is a membership-based club, it's open to the public every day the club is open because it's also a museum. In addition to a permanent collection of 1,800 works, the Society hosts special exhibitions throughout the year, weekly nude sketch nights, and themed sketch nights ranging from burlesque to boxing.

The Society's first monthly dinners in the early 20th century were attended by esteemed illustrators and personages like Mark Twain, Gloria Swanson, and N.C. Wyeth. The Cotton Club Band and Jimmy Durante performed here in the 1920s. The monthly brunches and dinners continue today in the dining room, with a charming historical bar, an outdoor patio and a rotating exhibition of artwork.

An original painting by Norman Rockwell, "The Christmas Coach", was donated to the club by the artist himself in 1935 and hangs above the bar. In Rockwell's description of the painting, he writes, "This painting now hangs in the clubhouse of the Society of Illustrators, New York. The bartender, Ted Croslin, is well known to illustrators, who are so fond of him that when he went to war they gave him a dinner. He is not as dour as he looks."

At the time, the bar at the Society was on the fourth floor. In the 1950s, the bar on the third floor was created and the Rockwell painting moved there in 2008. Above hangs a wooden crest from the dining table of LIFE Magazine illustrator Charles Dana Gibson.

The dining room fare is headed by Chef Q, who is known for his challah bread banana brûlée french toast and banana maple walnut syrup. The $30 brunch comes with a full buffet, coffee, tea, and a Mimosa, Bellini or Bloody Mary cocktail. The dinner, also a buffet, is $50. There's no official drink menu but you can ask the bartender for whatever strikes your fancy. One of the off-menu specialty cocktails that has stuck around is The F Train, consisting of organic cucumber vodka from Crop Earth, elderberry liqueur, lime juice, and pineapple juice.

THE STORAGE ROOM OF THE UES.

A unique ice-cream speakeasy

1707 2nd Avenue, Upper East Side, NY 10128
(646) 559-5889
theuesnyc.com
Tuesday to Friday 5pm–1am; Saturday 4pm–1am; Sunday 5pm–1am

This brightly painted dessert vendor isn't exactly incognito: UES. sticks out like a sore thumb on the Upper East Side (for which it is named) amid the toned-down, buttoned-up stores with which it shares its strip of Second Avenue. Outside, pink umbrellas and flower-garlanded stanchions surround heart-covered benches and purple chairs. Inside is no less lively, and those craving a scoop really can indulge – but there's a sweet secret to this storefront ice-cream parlor for those who can find it. Indeed, a whole other dimly lit world exists behind that extremely Instagram-worthy, pint container-covered wall.

To access the Storage Room, customers are tasked with finding the door. While the white bricked front is decked out in waffle-cone wallpaper and cotton-candy pink accents, a single step past the hinged pint display is a shrine-like bar for adults, with no children – or baseball caps, beanies, hoodies, athletic wear or "super casual wear" – allowed.

"At the time that I opened, we were the only ice-cream shop speakeasy in the world," claims Cortney Bond, who started UES. in 2017 after deciding that the notoriously stuffy neighborhood could use a little color. "I had a lot of interest in putting my concept downtown but wanted something for my hood," Bond – an Upper East Side resident herself – explains. "All of the cocktails are named after something that has to do with the Upper East Side and we have many ice-cream-themed cocktails for the guests to enjoy."

The vibe is decidedly modern, with intimate plush booths and stools for seating beneath a contemporary take on chandeliers and golden frames, many containing paintings, many without. The bar itself is far more than functional: the warmly backlit, columned centerpiece features three arched sets of shelves bursting with various booze bottles.

"I wanted guests to feel what it would feel like to be in a bar during Prohibition, so everything is dim, antique and sexy," says Bond.

In its five years slinging scoops and drinks in Manhattan's bougiest nabe, UES. has become a go-to oasis of upscale fun. "UES. was made by an Upper East Sider for Upper East Siders," says Bond, proudly adding that she firmly believes no other ice-cream speakeasy across the globe has executed the concept "quite like ours."

In 2024, Bond opened a similar concept downtown, on the Bowery. Called Champagne Problems, it's entered from a potato chip shop and contains a martini glass ball pit and Taylor Swift homages galore.

KEYS & HEELS

A top-notch cocktail bar behind a locksmith and a shoe repair

1488 2nd Avenue, Upper East Side, NY 10075
(917) 557-0217
keysandheels.com
Wednesday to Saturday, 6pm "til late"

Behind the disguise of a locksmith and a shoe repair claiming to have been cutting keys and fixing leather since 1971, Keys & Heels serves up top-notch cocktails in stylish surroundings.

"It was important to me to have an old New York City exterior that people would overlook, and yet when you enter, it transports you into another world," says founder Massimo Lusardi of his most recent venture on 2nd Avenue. (The speakeasy-style haunt is his third venue between 77th and 78th Streets; the other two – Uva and Uva Next Door – are next door.)

Although the fake front makes the restaurant more of a speakeasy than many bars that purport to be one, Lusardi decided to move away from the oft-used Prohibition aesthetic, instead going with a rich color palette and plush velvet for a more flirty, playful vibe.

There's a limited menu of lounge bite food offerings, including homemade focaccia, salmon tartare cones and marinated olives, but the focus is unabashedly on the two-part house cocktail list.

"Most places find that their house cocktails are popular for the first round, and then people order their usual favorites, but we have found people coming back over and over for our house cocktails," Lusardi proudly reports. Highlights include the Pretty Little Psycho (a "spicy af margarita"), the rye whiskey-based Upper East Side ("an uptown Manhattan") and a "fruit-forward margarita" called the Adulting. There are also bottle service offerings, wine and a limited selection of $9 beers.

As for the locksmith and cobbler services, leave your keys and shoes at home: the convincing storefront is entirely a gimmick, although Lusardi says it's worked so well that many passersby seem to believe it … probably because of the weathered-looking over-awning sign's claim that the shop has served the neighborhood's shoes and doors for decades.

"We make keys," a neon centered in the display window lies. That much is immediately obvious upon entering: the shtick continues slightly past the storefront, with patrons entering a closet-sized lobby, the kind of aging shoe-repair-related images you'd find in an actual cobbler affixed to its gray walls, before passing through another door and into the main space.

Not only are broken kicks unwelcome, but a dress code strictly disallows running shoes, flip-flops, baseball caps and beanies. Although the layout is intended to create private nooks to share the evening more intimately with your party, everyone is expected to look decent while doing it.

THE 2ND FLOOR

A bar hidden behind a kosher delicatessen

2nd floor of 1442 1st Avenue, Upper East Side, NY 10021
(212) 737-1700
2ndfloor.com
Thursday 5pm–12am, Friday and Saturday 5pm–2am

Since 1954, the Second Avenue Deli has been serving New Yorkers certified-kosher Jewish delicatessen offerings. And since 2017, 2nd Floor Bar & Essen – Yiddish for "to eat" – has been serving a finger food-ified version of its now certified-classic menu on the floor above it.

Stay downstairs for the full hot pastrami sandwich experience in homey booths and the classic clatter of a bustling Big Apple diner beneath bright lights and a tin ceiling; but for a more millennial-friendly experience, find the separate entrance on East 75th St. between 1st and York avenues and head upstairs for pastrami deviled eggs, pastrami popcorn, crispy pastrami mini- burgers and beet horseradish-stuffed gefilte croquettes in a dimly lit, sultry speakeasy space.

Thirsty? The delightfully Jewish deli-inspired cocktail menu includes the Upper Eastsider (an "uptown" take on the classic Moscow mule) and certified-kosher espresso martinis and piña coladas. No longer offered but not forgotten: The Man-O-Manischewitz.

The happy hour special offers the uniquely high-brow old-school option of any house cocktail and a half sandwich from downstairs for $29 (the 2nd Floor and the first both share a kitchen while maintaining mostly separate menus). For franks in a blanket or rugalach, either eatery can assist.

To get to the 2nd Floor, follow the old-timers into the deli and then locate the stairs or look for the door around the corner and head in and up.

While the original restaurant remains a gregarious New York landmark, the upstairs is better suited for a swanky first date, or even a wedding – it has hosted a few, and there are also party spaces within the bar for smaller private events. Indeed, for those who find themselves on the Upper East Side and want to go to neither a sports bar nor a classic white tablecloth joint, 2nd Floor Bar & Essen offers a wonderful alternative in a part of town where ambiance choice is relatively limited.

Despite its name, 2nd Avenue Deli is today located at 1442 1st Avenue, and there's also a second location at 162 East 33rd Street, although no speakeasy tops the latter. While it first opened on 2nd Avenue, a landlord dispute ended its half-century run in that original East Village location back in 2006, a decade after the restaurant's founder, Abe Lebewohl, was fatally shot on a bank run in 1996. The case remains unsolved, but Lebewohl's legacy lives on in not just the two current locations of 2nd Avenue Deli, but also a park named in his honor catty-corner from the original deli location, which is today a Chase Bank.

EMPLOYEES ONLY

Art Deco speakeasy behind a psychic sign

510 Hudson Street, West Village, NY 10014
(212) 242-3021
employeesonlynyc.com
Daily 6pm–4am
Palm reading and tarot cards from 7pm on
1 train/Christopher St
Moderate

If you've ever strolled through the West Village, you've probably noticed the proliferation of psychic shops, though it's rare to see people going in and out of them. If it weren't for the perpetual lines, it

would be easy to bypass the door on Hudson Street near Christopher Street with the neon psychic sign in the window. But those who do might never know that hidden inside is an award-winning cocktail bar and restaurant. Push aside the red velvet curtain in the vestibule, where an actual psychic reads palms and tarot cards from 7pm on, and you'll find yourself in a gorgeous bar.

The details are all Art Deco here. Wall panels are curved mahogany, a three-tiered ceiling molding draws the eye upward, where pendant lamps hang. The backbar's inch-thick glass shelves glow greenish along the edges, and the liquor bottles lined up are illuminated from behind. Opposite the curved brass bar, a few tables are positioned along the wall, where reproductions of '20s and '30s-era paintings and photographs by artists like Man Ray, Tamara de Lempicka, and Juan Gris hang with museum-style lights above them. There are vintage suitcases poised on a shelf over a beveled mirror, and a small metal fan in the corner. Before Employees Only opened in 2004, this space was Caffe Sha Sha. Back in the 1920s, it was a funeral parlor, and the marble floors are from that period. The fireplace, now framed by thick shiny metal, dates back to the building's original construction in the 1860s.

Behind the bar, bartenders elegantly dressed in white shake complex cocktails. There are classics, EO takes on the classics, and originals, like the Mata Hari, a blend of Remy Martin 1783 Cognac shaken with chai-infused Martini Rosso and pomegranate juice. After a bout of vigorous shaking, the bartender pours the concoction through a Hawthorne strainer into a coupe, and garnishes it with rosebuds. The drink is subtly sweet, smooth, and delightful. Many of the cocktail recipes change seasonally, so the Ginger Smash, made with fresh cranberries in winter, might be served with pineapple in summer.

In the back room, elevated by a few steps, guests dine on oysters, steak tartare (hailed as the best in the city), bacon-wrapped lamb chops, and ricotta gnocchi. In the back, there's a bit more space to get comfortable, with pale yellow banquettes and tables. On a shelf positioned high on the wall, the owners' collection of vintage shakers, mixers, and seltzer bottles holds court. After midnight, the kitchen switches over to a late-night menu, which features the kind of dishes you might crave after a long night of drinking – truffled grilled cheese with parmesan fries, chicken schnitzel, and Balkan street sausage, among them. The kitchen stays open until 3am, and at 3:30am they play Tom Waits and serve a free cup of chicken soup to the last brave souls in the bar – often service industry professionals who come for a nightcap after their shift. "When we opened, there wasn't a place where you could finish your shift and come for a good cocktail, a good meal, and have fun. We tried to tie it all up," says co-founder Igor Hadzismajlovic.

ANGEL'S SHARE

A Japanese-style craft cocktail bar and neo-speakeasy pioneer

45 Grove Street, West Village, NY 10014
angelssharenyc.com
Tuesday to Saturday 5pm on

On a tony Greenwich Village side street, on the ground floor of a sunken-entranced landmark at 45 Grove, is an early pioneer of Manhattan's neo-speakeasy and craft cocktail scene: Angel's Share.

There is no signage for Angel's Share, and once down the stairs and through the front door, patrons find themselves in a small and charming if purgatorial lobby. (Reservations are not taken, and customers should expect at least a brief wait to get in.)

Once inside, visitors are greeted by the bar's *pièce de résistance*, a hand-painted mural displaying Michelangelo's cherubs on the left and right, and a little angel with devil's horns in the center.

The name Angel's Share is in reference to the mural, which refers to an old saying coined by Scotch makers: When aging whisky, a small portion generally evaporates through the porous barrels during the process. That disappeared bit, Scotch makers would say, was the angels taking their share.

The menu offers a little history of the 31-year-old destination and its expectations of patrons. "Rules & etiquette established in 1993 still apply: no standing, no more than 4 people per party, no split parties," reads the menu.

The grand and storied building at 45 Grove, meanwhile, is far older. It was constructed first, in 1830, as a mansion, and then transformed, in 1871, into an apartment building, with visits from the likes of actors, including John Wilkes Booth, along the way.

It is actually the bar's second incarnation. From 1993 to 2022, Angel's Share was located east and a hair north, on the second-floor of the East Village's 8 Stuyvesant Street, up the stairs and through the unmarked door to the left of the sushi counter in the now shuttered Japanese restaurant Village Yokocho.

After almost three decades at that address, there was a landlord dispute, and Angel's Share closed. A rather desperate search and a brief summer as a pop-up ensued.

"I was really about to give up when I found this space," Erina Yoshida, daughter of Angel's founder Tony Yoshida, told The New York Times in March 2023, shortly before the bar reopened on Grove Street that July. "It had this Old World charm and a history, which was very important to me, knowing that we've been around for a long time, too."

Some things have changed since the reopening: In addition to the new location, Angel's Share now has a website and merchandise (vintage-wash baseball caps, t-shirts and tote bags, available for purchase behind the bar).

The namesake mural, however, is the same, as is the general ambiance and the offering of a chic, Japanese-style space to appreciate quality cocktails.

SUSHI BY BOU

"It has to be either behind something, under something or above something."

Multiple locations
info@sushibybou.com
sushibybou.com

This omakase speakeasy chain has got the art of hidden high-end sushi restaurants down to a formula.

Sushi By Bou founder Richie Romero and his partners came up with the idea of using small, unutilized corners of existing businesses to build-out humble but luxe dining spaces.

"It has to be hidden and it can't be prime real estate – it has to be either behind something, under something or above something," said Romero. "That's the whole premise, and we want it to always be a thousand square feet at the biggest."

To date, Sushi By Bou has nearly 30 locations spread across New Jersey, Illinois, Florida, Tennessee, and Puerto Rico.

In New York alone there are numerous locations (one in Westhampton and two upstate, the rest in Manhattan), each offering a slightly different set-up and menu.

Multiple Manhattan locations are currently in hotels: At E 32nd Street's Nomad NYC there's an intimate sushi counter inside an unmarked upper floor hotel room and at Times Square's Sanctuary Hotel there's a Sushi By Bou covered in colorful Japan-inspired murals, and providing vegan omakase.

In Greenwich Village there's Fins and Scales, offering a 13-course certified kosher omakase meal tucked inside a Chabad, and behind Chelsea's Super Nice Coffee there's a Sushi By Bou with the option of a signature 12-course omakase meal or a "Bougie" 17-course one.

"Chelsea's my favorite, personally," said Romero. "People get lost, which is the best part, 'cause they go in there and they go 'oh, this isn't Sushi By Bou.'" But it is: At the end of the counter in the florist-coffee shop front, beneath neon lights, a door leads to a hallway, which leads to Sushi By Bou's space, a swankily-decorated windowless room containing two high-top seating areas and assorted tables beneath a multitude of chandeliers.

For those looking for a top-of-the-line sushi meal, look elsewhere: Sushi By Bou does not pretend to be the best of the best when it comes to the quality of its food – that would be far more expensive than its $65 12-course offering. What it does claim to be, across locations, is the most bang for your buck omakase, with a lightly varied shtick and vibe that is consistently fun to find and experience.

Said Romero, "I call it 'affordable luxury.'"

DIN DIN SUPPER CLUB

A nomadic dinner pop-up that feels different than a restaurant

(484) 682-7814
dindinnyc.com - rezzos@dindinnyc.com

This nomadic dinner pop-up seems to garner a loyal following wherever it may go. Born in Portland, Oregon, Din Din started as a public supper club before getting a permanent home in 2013. Then, in 2016, owner and chef Courtney Sproule shuttered the space. The nine-year-old project, which has been credited with doing no less than reimagining the city's restaurant scene, had "come to fruition," she announced at the time.

It was big news for Portland foodies, with PDX Monthly describing Din Din's meals "as if Julia Child had joined the riot grrrl movement" and other local publications loudly lamenting the loss of the brick-and-mortar venue when it closed.

Sproule subsequently relocated to New York and restarted the venture, following the winds of opportunity and open space. Since moving to the boroughs, Din Din has inhabited a Lower East Side art gallery and a bitty retail store at the end of a row of eateries in Williamsburg.

The multicourse meals served at the events lean towards regional French cuisine "with aggressive, seasonal flavors presented with a modern, feminine hand," according to one flier for an upcoming dinner in Bed-Stuy. It's not only the quality of the food that has earned Sproule a following despite her lack of location and long-term scheduling, but also the promise of leisure, quality conversation and good wine as a pairing to the multicourse dinner. Din Din meals are generally dispensed family-style, on house-made plates, and feature two seatings. Attendance costs $90, gratuity included. Other upcoming events have both prix-fixe dinners and à la carte small plates with such offerings as lamb hazelnut crepinette and oyster ceviche.

"Guests often comment that Din Din feels different than a restaurant. This is the goal – we want our guests to feel at home and like they're a part of an evening that won't ever be repeated," says Sproule. "As a diner, I never want a good meal to end – I could stay at the table forever." The table, she says, quoting her mentor Chef Robert Reynolds, should be more than just a serving board for sustenance but "an excuse to come together."

"One of my favorite jobs as a chef is writing menus that honor the beauty of the table," says Sproule. "The harmony of a menu written with a sense of place, the grace of an arched meal designed to gently land you on your feet."

ALPHABETICAL INDEX

It was September 1995 and Thomas Jonglez was in Peshawar, the northern Pakistani city 20 kilometres from the tribal zone he was to visit a few days later. It occurred to him that he should record the hidden aspects of his native city, Paris, which he knew so well. During his seven-month trip back home from Beijing, the countries he crossed took in Tibet (entering clandestinely, hidden under blankets in an overnight bus), Iran and Kurdistan. He never took a plane but travelled by boat, train or bus, hitchhiking, cycling, on horseback or on foot, reaching Paris just in time to celebrate Christmas with the family.

On his return, he spent two fantastic years wandering the streets of the capital to gather material for his first "secret guide", written with a friend. For the next seven years he worked in the steel industry until the passion for discovery overtook him. He launched Jonglez Publishing in 2003 and moved to Venice three years later.

In 2013, in search of new adventures, the family left Venice and spent six months travelling to Brazil, via North Korea, Micronesia, the Solomon Islands, Easter Island, Peru and Bolivia. After seven years in Rio de Janeiro, he now lives in Berlin with his wife and three children.

Jonglez Publishing produces a range of titles in nine languages, released in 40 countries.

FROM THE SAME PUBLISHER

ATLAS

Atlas of abandoned France
Atlas of extreme weather
Atlas of forbidden places
Atlas of geographical curiosities
Atlas of geographical curiosities - Britain
Atlas of unusual wines

SECRET ATLAS

London - The secret atlas
New York - The secret atlas
Paris - The secret atlas
Venice - The secret atlas

PHOTO BOOKS

Abandoned America
Abandoned Asylums
Abandoned Australia
Abandoned Belgium
Abandoned Churches: Unclaimed places of worship
Abandoned cinemas of the world
Abandoned France
Abandoned Germany
Abandoned Italy
Abandoned Japan
Abandoned Lebanon
Abandoned Spain
Abandoned USSR
Abandoned world – An AI-generated exploration
After the Final Curtain – The Fall of the American Movie Theater
After the Final Curtain – America's Abandoned Theaters
Baikonur – Vestiges of the Soviet space programme
Cinemas – A French heritage
Clickbait – A visual journey through AI-generated stories
Forbidden France
Forbidden Places – Vol. 1
Forbidden Places – Vol. 2
Forbidden Places – Vol. 3
Forgotten France
Forgotten Heritage
Oblivion
Parisian Theatres
Secret sacred sites
Venice deserted
Venice from the skies

'SOUL OF' GUIDES

Soul of Amsterdam
Soul of Athens
Soul of Barcelona
Soul of Berlin
Soul of Brussels
Soul of Detroit
Soul of Kyoto
Soul of Lisbon
Soul of Los Angeles
Soul of Marrakesh
Soul of Marseille
Soul of Milan
Soul of New York
Soul of Paris
Soul of Rome
Soul of Tokyo
Soul of Venice
Soul of Vienna

'SECRET' GUIDES

Secret Amsterdam
Secret Bali – An unusual guide
Secret Bangkok
Secret Barcelona
Secret Bath – An unusual guide
Secret Belfast
Secret Berlin
Secret Boston – An unusual guide
Secret Brighton – An unusual guide
Secret Brooklyn – An unusual guide
Secret Brussels
Secret Budapest
Secret Buenos Aires
Secret Campania
Secret Cape Town
Secret Copenhagen
Secret Corsica
Secret Dolomites
Secret Dublin – An unusual guide
Secret Edinburgh – An unusual guide
Secret Florence
Secret French Riviera
Secret Geneva
Secret Glasgow
Secret Granada
Secret Helsinki
Secret Istanbul
Secret Johannesburg
Secret Kuala Lumpur
Secret Lisbon
Secret Liverpool – An unusual guide
Secret London – An unusual guide
Secret London – Unusual bars & restaurants
Secret Los Angeles – An unusual guide
Secret Louisiana – An unusual guide
Secret Madrid
Secret Mexico City
Secret Milan
Secret Montreal – An unusual guide
Secret Naples
Secret New Orleans – An unusual guide
Secret New York – An unusual guide
Secret New York – Curious activities
Secret New York – Hidden bars & restaurants
Secret Normandy
Secret Paris
Secret Potsdam
Secret Prague
Secret Provence
Secret Rio de Janeiro
Secret Rome
Secret Seville
Secret Singapore
Secret Stockholm
Secret Strasbourg
Secret Sussex – An unusual guide
Secret Tokyo
Secret Tuscany
Secret Venice
Secret Vienna
Secret Washington D.C. – An unusual guide
Secret York – An unusual guide

Follow us on Facebook and Instagram

PHOTO CREDITS
All photographs by Augustin Pasquet, Michelle Young and Alix Piorun

Layout: Emmanuelle Willard Toulemonde – **Translation:** Caroline Lawrence – **Correction:** Jana Gough – **Proofreading:** Abigail Kafka – **Publishing:** Clémence Mathé

In accordance with regularly upheld French jurisprudence (Toulouse 14-01-1887), the publisher will not be deemed responsible for any involuntary errors or omissions that may subsist in this guide despite our diligence and verifications by the editorial staff.
Any reproduction of the content, or part of the content, of this book by whatever means is forbidden without prior authorisation by the publisher.

© JONGLEZ 2025
Registration of copyright: October 2025 – Edition: 03
ISBN: 978-2-36195-758-2
Printed in Bulgaria by Dedrax